Flying Without A Net

The true story of a boy who defies all odds and runs away with Cirque du Soleil

VITAL GERMAINE

Flying Without A Net

Part 1

VITAL GERMAINE

Editior: Leslie Hoffman
Proofer: Lorraine Stalians
Cover: Maxwell Alexander Drake
Interior Design: Audrey Balzart

ISBN: 978-1-936525-85-0

www.iqpublishers.com

Printed in the United States of America

Flying Without A Net

One day I'm going to fly without a net.

CHAPTER 1

Las Vegas, Treasure Island Hotel, 1996
Cirque du Soleil's Mystère

A loud aerial clunk and collective gasp of fear resonated in the crowd. The horrendous cracking sound echoed around the theater above the volume of the music. Two human rag-dolls plummeted to earth. The two high-bar flyers, Vasily and Boris, lay motionless in the net.

As always, I watched the high bar act from behind the wings with my colleague, Philippe. Most nights went smoothly—timing compliant to a perfectly tuned Swiss watch. Flyers swiveled around their respective structures at opposite ends of the stage, set to hurl themselves twenty-five feet through thin air with no strings attached, all the while flipping. Occasionally, a flyer would fall into the net and have to regroup while the act continued. He'd climb up the rope ladder and reset. Tonight's fall was very different, however.

"Zey are way off," Philippe said with his pronounced French Canadian accent.

"Ah, so what. Same shit, different show. They know what to do," I responded. "They'll adjust, or fall; no big deal."

They made no attempt to adjust.

"*Merde*, shit!" gasped Philippe. "*Merde!* This not good."

We both stood up in disbelief, staring at the two bodies lying still in the undulating net.

Merde!

"Oh crap," Philippe said.

"What the --."

"*Non!*"

About ten seconds elapsed after the loud collision. Still no indication of life. Ten seconds of nothingness on stage is equal to about thirty minutes in normal life.

Another ten seconds passed. Still nothing. The only movement in the theater came from the musicians' fingers melodically pounding their instruments, vamping to lighten the gravity of the tragedy. Everybody knew it was serious, including the audience.

The cast had no choice but to remain focused and professional. Several of us went on stage and improvised in the hope of distracting the crowd. The director had prepared us for a moment like this with what he called "save the show," when performers executed unscripted choreography to camouflage a major malfunction.

We spied each other from the corner of our eyes to find a semblance of unison. Our counterfeited choreography couldn't disguise the weight of the motionless bodies. How long could we fake it?

"We need to get off the stage," yelled Mike, the dance captain.

We exited. Communication frenzy invaded the backstage area, headsets on overload. Decisions had to be made quickly. The show had never been stopped before. Incessant seconds circulated. Every tick increased the odds of a catastrophe. All turned still, other than the clock.

The technicians eased the safety net down. The music came to a confused halt.

The lead physical therapist, Karen, and the Cirque-trained EMTs entered the stage, stepped onto the net, and approached the motionless bodies to evaluate the situation. The sound of murmured curiosity and anxious heartbeats of hope saturated the theater.

I observed from the wings and noticed some guests had joined their palms and bowed their heads in silent prayer.

I'm glad it's not me, I thought selfishly, knowing tragedy could hit any one of us at any given moment.

Karen stabilized the acrobats' heads with great care. There could be a spinal cord injury. Non-stabilization of the head could mean the difference between a close call and paralysis. Fifteen hundred pairs of eyes scrutinized her every gesture, but she carried the incredible responsibility beyond reproach. Not to mention her colleagues' lives in her hands.

The paramedics where summoned to their first emergency. They waited outside at every show, in anticipation of such a moment. They came on stage with plenty of equipment and continued the evaluation. The deafening quiet in the theater sustained its volume.

The motionless fallen heroes were placed onto stretchers and carried off to applause.

This whole scene was one of most surreal moments I have ever encountered in the world of entertainment, if not in my life. More than the clocks of Dalí melted that night—time itself melted.

Backstage, morale hit an all time low. Wits trembled. The high-bar acrobats had all the while been hanging from their rig at sixty feet. They sat or stood on nothing more than thin metal piping of the high bars without the safety of the net. The long drop to earth had they tired slipped or lost concentration, would have been fatal.

In due time, the net reclaimed its taut status and the musicians regrouped.

Two, three, four. The drum rolled, the rest of the band followed. Everybody returned to their station. The show went on, as it must, though nervously. It ended with the customary standing ovation. This time, with a hint of apprehension in both the faces of the cast and of the audience.

They all witnessed a once-in-a-lifetime incident and at the regular price. As the final note of the reprise sounded and the house lights came on, the crowd made its way to the exits. They never knew the outcome of the two wounded warriors and, perhaps, still wonder today.

The performers gathered backstage and exchanged their worries, perspectives, and concerns. Questions and comments overlapped from all angles in disorder.

"Did you hear that sound?"

"Oh my God, everybody heard it."

"Don't be silly, it wasn't that bad."

"That sound was broken bone, dude."

"I think he fractured his skull."

News arrived from the hospital. The injuries weren't as bad as anticipated. Vasily had broken a leg in the thundering midair collision. He would need surgery and months of rehab. Boris was diagnosed with possessing a head made of Russian steel that had broken his partner's leg. He recovered from the concussion and returned to the show within days.

They both defied death that night and lived to fly another day.

CHAPTER 2

The next day, I clocked-in as usual, signing my name on the attendance sheet. A notice board by the entrance of the production office announced all changes and absences for that night's show. As expected, Vasily and Boris would not perform.

I headed down the long, unwelcoming, yellow hallway to the darkness of the narrow backstage passageways.

"Hey, Jennifer. How was your weekend?" I said to the long blond-haired lighting tech.

"Could have been better, could have been worse. Have a good show."

We carefully slid by each other.

I continued down the obscure path that ran the length of backstage, opened the door to the dressing room, and greeted my colleagues.

We briefly talked about yesterday's events, trivial stuff, joked and threw in a complaint here and there about company politics and one or two ass-holes in the show. Business as usual.

With the help of make-up, I physically and mentally transitioned into a being from another world. I would need to be prepared to fly, spin, and defy death and gravity above the audience on bungee trapeze. People have died from bungees and trapezes before, given, not in *Mystère*.

"Stand by, five minutes, *attention, cinq minutes*. Places please," announced the stage manager over the PA system. SHOW TIME!

CHAPTER 3

The overture began. Lights swept across the space. Fat blue and white *Spermato* characters chased the clown, Benny, across the stage and through the aisles. Taiko drums descended from cables with seated artists pounding the skins. Beats bellowed around the theatre. Brightly colored characters appeared onto the slowly rising psychedelic colored stage. They danced, flipped, jumped, and ran in eccentric ways. The music ended on a crescendo, leaving only the big-bellied baby, Francis, with his large, bouncy, red ball.

His innocent high-pitched voice caused plenty of laughter. The rest of his opening act created even more.

A sequence of minor cues and a visit to the physio department for treatment kept me busy between the overture and my main act, bungee trapeze.

"Don't forget to ice your shoulder after bungee, Vital," said Janice, the therapist on duty.

"Yeah, my favorite," I replied, and headed to the dressing room to change into the bungee trapeze costume.

All my bungee teammates inside went quiet and serious for a second.

"What's up?" I asked.

"Oh, nothing, we're just tired," one girl answered.

"Who used Tiger Balm? It stinks!" I said.

All the girls looked at each other then burst out laughing.

"Yeah, you're tired all right. Whatever," I responded. They left. I turned to my *NewYoRican* bungee partner, Chris. "Yo, wos with the girls today?"

"Ah, you know girls, dude. Anyway, have a fun show, bro." He exited with a grimace on his face.

Off came my *Laquai* costume, keeping only my G-string on. The men's bungee outfit covered very little, revealing plenty of flesh; nothing more than a jungle tie-dyed, spandex thong.

To complement the minimalist attire, I wore a very elaborate and heavy headpiece ordained with earth tone moldings. It looked as flamboyant as that of an exotic bird showing off at the peak of a mating ritual.

The matching wristbands and ankle accessories had strands of long twisted fabric to give it the feel of dangling seaweed. They reminded me of the audition when Debbie Brown had asked us to show her how smiling seaweed danced. A touch of sparkles here and there gave it glitz and glam. I looked like a tribal Vegas showgirl on steroids without the heels.

The bungee girl's costume had the same vibe, but made of a bright yellow full-body suit with hints of browns and reds. The ladies looked like poisonous jellyfish from the depths of an obscure exotic ocean.

I pulled my bungee thong over my G-string, and all other wardrobe parts followed. Lastly, on went the custom harness. I checked all safety features: clips fastened, straps tightened, and Velcro stuck. Aerialists can never be safe enough at Cirque. I walked out into the hallway and did my regular quick warm-up, a series of fifty push-ups and abdominal crunches before heading up to the tech ring. The smell of Tiger Balm lingered as if following me.

Behind the door to the tech ring on the fourth floor hid the charm and intrigue of *Mystère's* upper backstage. Being up so high gave an empowering sensation. I always took a moment to absorb and look down and observe the mesmerized expressions of the audience below. The theatrical lighting danced across their faces. All seats were full.

Barefoot, I climbed up the iron ladder to the catwalk, walking over the stage in darkness. To think, heights scared me when first joining Cirque. Elevations had now become commonplace and home.

At my spot, I checked my bungee chords, clipped them to my harness at my waist, and slid them over the railing. The technicians double-checked everything using small dim pocket flashlights to see. They attached me to a safety cable that connected to a chain motor. I climbed over the barrier and eased myself down until the wire became taut. Suspended sixty feet in the air looking straight down at rows 1 through 5 of section 102, I waited till it was time to descend.

All the while, the hypnotized audience watched the Hand Balancing act without a clue of our imminent descent. They were in complete awe of the two muscle men demonstrating beyond human strength, balance and agility atop a large brightly lit semi-dome. It had a feel of something out of the lost city of Atlantis. The top acrobat, midst a one-arm handstand on his partner's head, poised precariously using his parted legs as counter balance.

The Chilean technician, Waldo, pushed a button and lowered me down in silence like a Navy Seal sneaking up on the enemy. The guests seated below were in for a pleasant surprise, as was I.

Seconds later, my toes eased onto the trapeze. I steadied by wrapping my arms around the trapeze rope, then unclipped the safety cable, a tricky maneuver to execute. The safety cable slowly disappeared up into the void with stealth.

When the five other bungee artists came down, they nodded to acknowledge they had unclipped and were ready to fly. As team captain, the responsibility of safety and togetherness lay in my hands. We were cleared for takeoff.

But why are they all looking at me full of such grins? Unusual. They're supposed to be tired.

A tingle in my crotch distracted me.

The scent of Tiger Balm, the giggling girls, my sneaky smiling partner, and the growing heat between my legs aroused my suspicion.

But, of course. The joke was on me. It suddenly all made sense.

They had massaged the Tiger Balm into my thong and it had seeped through my G-string to my testicles.

Son's-a-bitches!

I bent my legs and opened my stance on the trapeze to allow better crotch ventilation, much to the amusement of my traitor colleagues.

The music changed. I squeezed my thighs shut and focused. The count off began. Two, three, four. On the count of five, I nodded to the group. They responded. On the next count of one, we all pushed our trapeze away with our foot and fell straight down to earth. After so many shows, the dead vertical drop still left my stomach tingling in my throat. It kept my abandoned inner child alive and happy.

We swooped down onto the unsuspecting audience. They gasped. The bungee cords stretched as the pressure in my crotch from the harness increased. We came so close to the guests, I could make out the details of their faces. The recoil of the bungee shot me back up to the trapeze like a space-bound rocket.

We did a series of choreographed moves, ending the introduction with a subtle bow. The applause and admiration from below were my favorite things. My heart beamed. My blood boogie-oogied.

By the all-but-last segment of the act, the Tiger Balm barbecued my testicles. They roared and drowned in their own perspiration.

Esti de Câllise! (Religious French Canadian slur).

As our trapezes swung in unison, we undulated our

bodies, giving in to the airstream that stroked our cheeks. The girls fluttered their feet. Chris and I shook our heads like proud stallions. When we all came to the center as one flower, I checked everybody's position and prepared to give the cue for the next choreographic sequence. I'd normally shout out "next" but, considering the circumstances, I made a minor change and yelled "hot" to add to the comedy.

Though I, Vital, was clearly the joke, we all got the last laugh. The act ended with the usual cheers and handclapping from the audience.

I loved this life and flying. As for the Tiger Balm, a quick visit to the men's room and several splashes of cold water helped sooth the discomfort. I prayed that no sperm were damaged. Such pranks kept the show alive and new, even if at my expense. Revenge is a bitch, however.

Watch your backs, bungee team!

On the way back to the dressing room, I stopped by Physio to ice my injured shoulder and catch my breath.

"Here as promised, Janice."

"How's your shoulder?"

"It hurts, but what's new?"

"Ice it immediately, then come and see me between shows for treatment."

I had tweaked a rotator cuff months ago, but it still bothered me. Healing was tough without a substantial break, and six shows a week left little time to recover. We just sucked up the pain, popped Ibuprofen and clenched our teeth. If we didn't hurt, it meant we were dead.

The dressing room sat empty. I had a moment of peace and quite and time to retouch my makeup and towel dry. I looked in the mirror and deep into my eyes, wondering how I had achieved this great dream of running away with the circus, but not just any circus, CIRQUE DU SOLEIL!

The reality of my upbringing, though not the poetry of Cirque du Soleil, embraced a circus of sorts. Yet, here I flew among the elite in one of the world's biggest and best shows. According to statistics, I should have been dead or in jail by the age of eighteen, due to gang related crime or violence.

How did I land on both feet and manage to defy the odds and still live my dream? Well, it seems that life is all about overcoming challenges in order to find success. So, do we overcome those challenges?

CHAPTER 4

The journey began in 1964. I was born to an African mother, Regina Tshilumba, and a Caucasian father, Eugene Jacob, in The Belgian Congo during a horrific civil war. My birth town, then called Stanleyville, is now Kisangani. It is located in the north about 800 miles from the capital of Kinshasa, formerly Leopoldville, where Muhammad Ali fought George Foreman in a classic Heavyweight-boxing bout better known as "The Rumble in the Jungle," which put the country on the map. Today, the country of Zaire is called The Democratic Republic of Congo.

I had two dark-skinned African half-brothers, Jean-Pierre and Rudy. They were the biological sons of my mother's first marriage. From his first marriage, my father had one son, Daniel, who suffered from multiple sclerosis. His mother was deceased. Daniel was born Caucasian. He lived safely in Brussels with Grandma and Grandpa, far away from the African skirmish that threatened me.

While my half-brother fought his own personal war against illness and paternal abandonment in Brussels, discontent brewed in the cities and jungles of the Congo. My family became caught in crossfire between *Niggers* and *Wouzoungous* (as the Congolese call Whites). The natives hungered for *Wouzoungou* scalps and justice, and my blue-eyed Caucasian father's blonde-haired scalp would do them just fine. All the while, Belgian paratroopers raided, raped, and pillaged towns with orders to kill Africans, such as my mother and my brothers, in order to save Belgian Nationals.

With angels on our side, we escaped when I was only six months old. We left everything behind: cousins, aunties, close family friends, Mum's thriving transportation enterprise, and a monkey named Gigi, who enjoyed feeding me from the bottle, apparently adopting me as her son.

Our flight took us to Belgium, where we united with Daniel and my grandparents. This was the first time they held me. We lived with Grandma and Grandpa in Brussels until I turned three.

Though too young to remember, the family portrait must have made for mishmash, hodgepodge conversation—two African boys, a Caucasian boy, a black mother, a white father, two white grandparents with silver hair and me, a Mulatto with ginger hair. We stood as colorfully psychedelic as the current fashion of the late sixties.

From Belgium, we journeyed briefly to Holland, then Fribourg, Switzerland for about six months, before moving to England permanently. We left Daniel behind with Grandma and Grandpa, and lived safely in London under the protection of the New Congolese Consulate.

Africa fell into the past. The British capital transformed into a new, promising start for us, offering peace, security, and delicious apple crumble with custard.

Hope filled my heart. Dream and aspirations established themselves in my mind. I believed everything was possible and couldn't wait for this new life to begin. Tomorrow was going to be wonderful.

CHAPTER 5

My first memories of London were not of Buckingham Palace, The Houses of Parliament, or Spam sandwiches, but of a small flat close to Oxford Street, a famous shopping destination in the city center. The address was 56 Welbeck Street. We resided on the ground floor—Mum, Dad, Jean-Pierre, Rudy, and me. We spoke French at home for the most part but, somehow, English became the norm. I don't remember learning.

Mum's African clout landed her a fantastic job at the New Congolese Consulate. She often took me to work. Dad stayed at home.

Mum must have been an important woman, because businessmen always surrounded her. They all carried attaché cases and wore impeccable suits and crisp dry-cleaned shirts with cufflinks. I liked to wear my cufflinks, too. They matched my tiny little suit and shiny black shoes. Mum attended many receptions and was often chauffeured in limousines. It felt so cool to ride in big black limousines. Mum taught me to be quiet and polite while with her. I only spoke when spoken to and stayed close to her for reassurance.

Life was good. Comfortable. Many perks.

Dad hated her job. Rarely did he attend the functions. It created tension between them. He often asked questions about what she did, and whom she talked to.

Once, I saw him search her purse. I knew it was wrong to pry, so I yelled out to Mum in the room next door.

"*Maman, Papa* is goin' through your purse."

They fought. It was my fault. I swore to never rat on anybody again, but I hated seeing Dad sneak through Mum's stuff, so I told her again the next time he did it.

Result: another fight.

The months passed quickly. Parental fights came and went. One day they'd laugh, kiss and love: next day they'd want to kill each other.

I didn't understand adults. So childish.

My brothers and I did what boys did. We played and had pretend fights with guns, or tried to do Kung Fu like Bruce Lee. We also dreamt of building a flying car like on *The Jetsons*.

I, personally, wanted to become a famous soccer player like Pele, or Georgie Best, a wizard of an Irish sensation that played for Manchester United, my favorite team. I wanted to play in the World Cup one day and score the winning goal for England, not Belgium or Africa.

If not soccer, then I wished to be a scientist, or maybe an astronaut or civil engineer. Law and journalism sounded cool, too.

Mum reminded us that school was priceless and to pay attention and learn. "Always respect teachers and adults, but never forget where you came from and what you believe in." Her lessons stuck.

The name of my school was St. Vincent's, a Catholic School run by nuns. It sat literally around the corner from our home on Welbeck Street. I got along with a lot of pupils and had many friends. They liked me because I was good at soccer and they wanted to play on my team.

I wish Mum and Dad would get along better and be a team.

Maybe the nuns could teach them about forgiveness and understanding, or simply bless the two of them. That way they would fight less and love more.

I'll pray for them tonight.

But the fights continued, grew more dangerous, sometimes turning into mean, ugly physical encounters. Objects flew. Things got smashed.

Jealousy and dishonesty were ugly things. That's all I saw and heard at home.

Why did people lie? It's silly and so much easier to tell the truth. My naïve mind had figured it out. I would solve the world's problems with love and honesty.

I only told white lies. They were harmless, so they weren't really lies, just fibs. Besides, the priest at confession forgave me for my sins, so that made them okay. That didn't seem right to me, but if God decided it was okay to sin if you asked for forgiveness, who was I to complain?

I should bring my parents to confession next time so they can learn to forgive like Jesus.

Another day, another disagreement, another fight between them. Their compressed tempers triggered off an emotional volcano that spewed verbal lava, punches and slaps.

"You're a liar," yelled Dad.

"No, listen," Mum replied.

"Shut your mouth you dirty, filthy slut. You deceived me."

Dad held Mum by the scruff of the neck. She gasped for air, all the while coughing and cursing. I can never seem to define the face that is my dad. It remains a shadow or a silhouette cloaked in mystery and darkness.

I didn't know where Rudy and Jean-Pierre were. I wished they were here.

"Stop! Please stop!" I begged Mum and Dad. "Dad, you're hurting Mum. Stop it please."

They ignored me and slipped and fell during the commotion. A head banged against the wall. One body tumbled to the ground.

Another scuffle. A hat with a shiny badge rolled to my feet. Dad's arms were tied behind his back with some metal wrist bracelets. From nowhere, a woman police officer held Mum back. I couldn't tell if Mum was furious at the police or at Dad, probably both. Dad yelled in French.

"Take your hands off of me, you bastards. I've done nothing. Nothing! She's lying. Liar!"

Everyone except Mum vanished from the hall. The black front door banged shut, and the silhouettes disappeared into the frosted panes. Momentary silence deafened me. Car doors slammed outside. Engines accelerated into the distance, sirens blaring.

Only sniffles whispering from my nose reached my ears. I tried to be a man and not whimper, but I was afraid, confused and, maybe, even angry.

Mum cried. It made me sniffle even more. She lay seated on the floor with her back against the wall and her head down, her hair ruffled, face covered in mascara. I knelt next to her and held her hand, not because I needed comforting, but because I wanted to comfort her, to be strong for her.

"Don't cry Mum. It's over. Please don't cry, I'll take care of you," I told her.

Our family dynamics changed considerably in his absence. Mum's strength and grace wobbled. She carried a heavy burden that I was too young to comprehend, but aware enough to realize things would never be the same. I gave up on a wonderful tomorrow, but only for a few days. Mum would get over this. We'd get over this. At least I hoped we would.

We moved upstairs into a smaller, cheaper flat in the same house. Mum became distant, less patient, not as gentle. Her affectionate side turned its back to the sun, casting a long dramatic shadow. The smile that once lit up a son's world blackened to dusk. Her flame flickered for survival but suffocated instead.

Mum was breaking. No, she was broken!

Getting out of bed became an overwhelming chore. She forgot things. If she wasn't drinking the occasional Guinness—which she said was good for her health 'cause it's strong, she also loved to secretly drink Gin from a silver flask she hid in her purse.

She once gave me a swig from her flask to warm me up one winter day while waiting for a bus. It worked. My tongue throbbed, my chest burned, and I coughed repeatedly. The cold faded. Mum was right. Then I felt funny in the head. Mum laughed.

Happy moments sporadically lighted up the darkness of reality, but they were short lived and few and far between. I savored each one, but worried that one day they'd disappear forever.

"Stop worrying," Jean-Pierre told us. "Everything's gonna be all right. Mum's just not well right now."

Rudy appeared doubtful. It was obvious to see in his eyes.

I remained hopeful. I wanted to believe Jean-Pierre.

"How much longer will it be, Jean-Pierre? I miss the old days."

"Soon, Vital, soon."

Mum suffered a nervous breakdown and lost her job. No more rides in the cool black limousines. No need to shine my Sunday shoes anymore, because we're not going anywhere special. My cufflinks collected dust in their velvet box. My suit grew too small.

With nothing more to lose and even less to hide, Mum openly drowned her anguish in the non-judgmental company of alcohol. Empty bottles littered everywhere. The house was a mess. Her once lovely clothes lay wrinkled on the bed or discarded on the floor in the corner of the room.

Her cheeks lost their tang, and her eyes drifted vacantly like those of a sad clown without a fake, painted smile. I couldn't remember the last time she wore lipstick or eye shadow, let alone a smile.

It hurt to watch Mum lose her dignity—and wither to a living skeleton with greyish skin and breath that constantly reeked of alcohol. First, no more Dad. Now, no more Mum. *What did we do to deserve this? It might all be my fault. I should've never told Mum about Dad.*

It is all my fault.

CHAPTER 6

We moved again to an even cheaper furnished flat a couple of miles away in Kensington, on Russell Road. We lived in a very somber basement. The hallway bulb didn't have a shade and emitted a gloomy yellow light. A moldering wire connected it to a flaking ceiling.

Mum slept on the living room's dull and forgettable sleeper couch. A record player sat on a small stand. Below it, a box filled with seven-inch and ten-inch vinyls. Though not allowed to touch, I knew how to stack the records, which buttons to push, and how to clean the needle. I learned by watching Mum. The ten-inch records played at 78 rpm, the smaller ones at 45, and LPs played at 33.

Some of her records were French, in particular, a few by Charles Aznavour, and the beautiful Françoise Hardy.

Ah, Françoise, my first crush.

I enjoyed staring at her picture on the cover and pretended she would marry me one day. Mum thought it cute and teased me about it.

"Ooh la la, Françoise. Je t'aime, Françoise Hardy."

Mum was in love with Elvis. I teased her back with a lip curl.

"I said a one for the money, thank you. Uh, thank you very much."

I wanted to be a singer like him one day. My favorite Elvis records were *In the Ghetto* and *Suspicious Minds*. I knew all the words. They made me sad, though, reminding me of Dad. He had a suspicious mind, and we're probably living in the ghetto because of him.

The reddish brown carpet in the living room had a square pattern. Its design fit perfectly for use as fake streets when playing with my car collection. Mattel had the best cars with nifty wheels and doors that actually opened. There were probably forty-five cars, if not more, in my collection, including a black taxicab and a dark green MGB, and one big fat black American car like in Hawaii Five-O.

"I'm gonna live in America one day, Mum, and drive a big car. I'll take you wherever you want."

"You're very kind, *Tonton.*"

Story had it that *Tonton* was the first word I ever spoke. It stuck with me as a nickname. It means uncle in Swahili.

The Belgians also used it as a term of endearment, as well as uncle. I liked the name *Tonton.* It made me feel special and loved.

"Take me to Hawaii?" Mum asked.

"Lovely. I'll be your chauffeur and wear a black hat."

"You can't even see over the steering wheel, *Tonton,*" she said with a smile.

"Can I wear my suit and cufflinks?"

"Even better, we'll get you a brand new tailor-made suit, new shoes, and plenty of starched shirts."

"What about a bike? A racing bike with ten gears. Can we go and eat fancy dinners in chic restaurants?"

"Yes, we can, if Jack Lord is there."

"Ooh la la, Monsieur Jacque."

"We'll do everything and anything, my sweet little boy."

She hugged me. It brought me joy, and I played with my cars. Mum got a drink. That brought her joy.

The cars kept me entertained and stimulated my imagination. I created a complete city with traffic jams, robbery escapes, chases, and crashes.

One day, when we have money again, I hope to get a Lima train set, too.

I fantasized a lot and was addicted to my dream world. Reality reminded me we were poor, hungry, and broke. I remembered Jean-Pierre's words of encouragement for strength.

"Soon, Vital, soon."

I need to be patient, I told myself. A voice deep inside told me all would be well if I just believed.

Next to Mum's bed dwelled the liquor cabinet, her sanctuary. It overshadowed the old brown out-of-tune piano. Rudy played it quite well. I could feel his passion and pain. He played sad songs and wrote his own love ballads. Jean-Pierre didn't seem to know the piano existed. He acted too cool and too logical to show emotion like Rudy.

He called Rudy a sensitive soul.

I think I'm sensitive, too, 'cause I feel a lot.

"Feelings are for sissies, *Tonton*!" Jean-Pierre clarified. "Real men join the army and don't feel."

"Is that why you love the Army cadets so much?"

"Of course. Soldiers are not trained to think, but programmed to follow orders and do things with courage."

"So does that mean I don't have courage? What about imagination? Do soldiers have imagination or just guns and grenades?"

"What do you think, *Tonton*. Use your imagination."

"Why do you always have to be a smart ars, Sergeant Major Jean-Pierre?"

They once took me to visit the Army cadets. The drills were fun to watch, but I still preferred my imagination and feelings to war. My brothers made me proud, though. They were so together with all the other soldiers. Their Sergeant even allowed me to give some orders. That made my day. I was the proudest and shortest make-believe corporal in the Royal Green Jackets.

"By the front, quick march! Left turn!"

They all followed my commands with precision.

"Left turn!"

I made them march in circles for hours, because I could only remember one or two orders.

Jean-Pierre planned to return to Belgium one day and join the *Gendarmerie* he told us. The *Gendarmerie* was a Belgian military unit with police-like responsibilities in the community. They no longer exist. He loved his cadets and their uniform. Rudy did, too, but not as much.

I liked the Scouts *and* my feelings. I was definitely not a sissy, though.

We had our own room and separate beds away from Mum. It was a great shame this flat was so dark and dirty. Worse still, a big rat resided somewhere in the kitchen. It scurried over the floor at night. It scared me. My brothers tortured me about it.

"We saw the rat get into your bed, *Tonton*. It's waiting for you at the bottom. It's gonna gobble you all up when you're asleep. Yum, yum. *Bon appetite.*"

"Get lost. Leave me alone."

I cried in secret and chose to sleep with Mum. My brothers told me it's all a joke, but I didn't believe them. After several talks, Mum convinced me otherwise. I loved it when she had those rare moments of patience and caring.

Even still, every noise in the house put me on edge.

"Soddin rat," I said. "The bloody thing's gotta go!"

We placed a trap in the corner of the kitchen by the dustbin and waited.

The snare caught its prey that same night—a minor victory. I felt like a man.

The beast was a greyish black, huge and ugly, with sharp jaundiced teeth and cold evil eyes that watched me, despite death. I avoided the kitchen for quite a while afterward, and my brothers teased me even more.

Guess I'm not quite a man yet, after all.

Ironically, we became just like the rat, desperately in search of grub, but there was none. My brothers and I stole food from a corner supermarket down the street. A growling stomach changes a young boy, if not a grown man.

We overcame and survived the hunger, growing from the experience. I understood that determination went a long way.

CHAPTER 7

The sixties ended. We sighed and gazed forward to the seventies.

I was now, six years old, the smallest kid in my class and awfully shy about my grin, with its two front teeth missing. As for my Afro, nobody had permission to touch it. Not even Mum.

Rudy was about twelve, and Jean-Pierre almost fourteen but looked and acted much older. People sometimes thought Mum and Jean-Pierre were lovers because he looked so old and she looked so young.

Another Christmas came and went. Meager presents exchanged as expected. I didn't like Christmas and have forgotten most of them. New Year's Eve was different.

One in particular stands out.

Mum allowed us to drink that night. I got giddy, Rudy tipsy, and Jean-Pierre drunk.

Jean-Pierre's typical ice-cold blood briefly warmed while under the influence of gin and orange. He had his customary toothpick in his mouth to look cool and, for a change, actually showed signs of a heart. The alcohol surged to his head, turning his normally quiet strength into anger and insolence.

He argued with Mum, confronting her negligence and irresponsibility. She was hurt by his verbal attack and knocked back several stiff drinks in short succession.

"Where are your manners?"

"Look at you, Mum. We don't deserve this."

"How dare you. I *am* your mother, Jean-Pierre Jacob."

"Then act like it."

"I beg your pardon! Who are you to judge? When I was your age, I was an adult already. I walked five miles to get water from a well in the middle of the jungle. You're not even half a man. I'm ill, and you can't even take care of me."

"You're a mess. Look at you. You're a pathetic alcoholic, not a parent. We're ashamed of you. We would have been better off with Dad."

We literally saw her swallow an oversized lump in her throat. Her eyes filled with sadness and blinked in frenzy. She emptied the final drops of gin from the bottle then chucked it at his head. He ducked, and it slammed against the wall without breaking. It spun on the floor.

Mum stumbled into her room, yelling in French, broken English, and Swahili. The door smashed shut and the apartment replied with a shudder. We didn't know what to do or what to say. With accusation written all over our faces, we eyed Jean-Pierre for a cue.

"What? Don't look at me like that. Oh, right, it's all Jean-Pierre's fault, *innit*?"

We remained silent.

"Oh, come off it guys, she just tried to kill me for Christ sake."

"Yeah, but you can't talk to Mum like that," Rudy replied.

"Oh, piss off! She's forgotten who she is. It's true. Just listen to her. She's so bloody drunk, she don't even know what she's bloody sayin' and what bloody language she's talking in. What am I supposed to do?"

Neither Rudy nor I responded. We simply watched him.

"I'm sick and tired of it. I'm always carrying the responsibility for every bloody thing. It's not my bloody job. I can't take care of myself, you two, and her, so leave me the fuck alone! Blame her, blame Dad, blame the gin, but don't...don't blame me."

He punched the wall. His anger remained unsatisfied, so he grabbed the broomstick and attempted to snap it in half across his knee. The effort failed, which only aggravated his growing fury. He jammed it between the table and a chair and, with one swift strike, karate chopped the broomstick in half.

"It's not my job to be in charge," he yelled. "I'm not your bloody mum, nor your dad. Who takes care of *me*, eh? Tell me, who takes care of Jean-Pierre? Nobody does, that's who."

"You okay, man," Rudy asked, with a calm voice.

"I didn't feel a thing. Nothing! I never feel anything. Ever!"

He flicked the toothpick out of his mouth, dropped to the floor, and began an endless series of push-ups on his fists, veins bulging from his forearms. He counted out loud till the end.

"Forty eight, forty nine, fifty!"

Jean-Pierre pushed himself from his fists onto his fingertips and started the count over.

"Sixteen, seventeen...."

"C'mon, Jean-Pierre!" Rudy shouted.

"Eighteen, nineteen...."

"You can do it!"

Twenty! My brother had just done twenty push-ups on his fingertips.

One day I'm gonna learn to do that, too.

Jean-Pierre caught his breath and jumped to his feet. Out came the Nunchakus. They skillfully whizzed around his body, under his armpits, and dangerously close to his head. I was in awe. Mesmerized.

"I could have punched a hole in that wall if I'd wanted to," he declared.

With clenched fists, he extended his right arm toward the wall and back to his body. His breaths grew deep and hypnotic, while he repeated the motion.

Swiftly, like over-stressed elastic, his punch snapped at lightning speed, followed by a grunt. This time, unlike the first punch, his knuckles disappeared into the wall as promised.

When he withdrew his fist, there wasn't a scratch on his skin.

"Sensei Jean-Pierre." Rudy encouraged him. "You're the black Bruce Lee, man."

Jean-Pierre strutted down the narrow hallway and kicked our bedroom door open. It warped and whacked against the wall.

"I've had enough!" Jean-Pierre bawled.

"Get Mum, *Tonton*," Rudy said to me.

I ran into Mum's room desperate for help. She lay passed out on her bed.

"Mum, Mum, wake up!" I shook her.

She mumbled, eyes closed, yet remained in her secure world of liquor and denial.

When I hurried back, Rudy was trying to diffuse the situation.

"Calm down, Jean-Pierre, calm down, man," he said. "Let it go. It's nobody's fault, man. Just calm down."

Jean-Pierre sat on the bed in silence, head down, and hands on his lap. We left him alone and cleaned up the hallway.

Minutes later, he came out in his Cadet uniform. His boots were clearly coated with spit and polish. The toecaps shone like mirrors, and his trousers were neatly tucked into muddy green spats with his beret tipped to one side. He booted his heel into the floor at attention and saluted us, then marched toward the front door. Gently, he opened it, leaving it ajar, and walked outside. We followed.

It felt nippy and was dark, with only a distant street lamp interrupting the night. We heard the sound of a squealing engine and a single flickering headlamp coming our way.

Jean-Pierre ran out onto the street.

"Come and get it, you bastards," he yelled. "You're breakfast. Beans on toast, and guess who's toast?"

The noise erupted from the oncoming two-stroke moped. Jean-Pierre slipped his belt from his trousers, lunged at the motorized bicycle, and swung his belt like a medieval flail at the poor old man who rode it. The old geezer swerved, skidded, and cursed a litany of words similar to those Mum and Dad used to say to each other when out of love.

"Come here and say that, you chicken feed sissy!" Jean-Pierre taunted back. "Come here, I dare ya! Come and chew my metal toecaps, you wanker."

"Yeah, you wolly, I double dare ya," I added in a high-pitched voice.

Slowly, the man's red taillight dissolved into the silent shadows followed by a swirling trail of grey exhaust.

Jean-Pierre beat his chest like a tribal warrior celebrating a kill. A penetrating exhale thundered from his chest.

To our surprise, Jean-Pierre laughed hard and loud. His snickering was contagious. Before long, we were all chortling from the depths of our cramping stomachs.

We larked around like kids without a worry into the morning. The sun rose, barely breaking the heavy cloud cover.

Nothing would ever happen to us on Jean-Pierre's watch, our fearless soldier. Of that I was sure.

I'd die for him.

CHAPTER 8

Happy New Year! Bonne Annee!

The decade began on an optimistic note, other than Mum waking up with a severe headache. She drank more Guinness to make it go away.

A week flew by, and we had yet to stop laughing about the moped incident.

We were enthusiastic that in nineteen seventy, life would be different. But no such luck. Mum drank more Guinness, and we ate less. I still went to the same old school, living the same old life. My school uniform hadn't changed, either. It's just a little more tattered. Father Christmas didn't bring me the new clothes I asked for. Concerning a bike, I gave up on that long ago. He also forgot to bring Dad back and make Mum stop drinking.

To be honest, the state of my uniform embarrassed me more than Mum's drinking. The elbows of my navy blue sweater needed stitching. My trousers had a hole in the knee and hung an inch or three too short. My shoes were scuffed, and the heels left much to be desired. The kids at school made snide remarks, sometimes. I ignored them as best I could.

Despite the shame, I still loved school. I could even get there on my own now, taking two London Transport red, double decker buses across town.

It's fun to sit upstairs, even though crowded and filled with smoke. During the ride I would gaze at the scurrying city ants with lackluster looks, carrying umbrellas. I could also tie my own tie and do my own shoelaces.

I don't think I even need Mum anymore.

The name of my school was Saint Vincent's Roman Catholic School for Boys and Girls. It's in Paddington. A carved shield hung above the gate that announced its name to all visitors. The gate was a large, intimidating black gothic device that connected to an iron railing. The railing circled the building like a deathly centurion warding off infidels.

Inside lay a large inner courtyard that acted as our playground during playtime. On the roof lay a caged-off yard designated for the higher grades. My two brothers snuck me up there once when they were still students there. We could see around for miles. I felt so cool up until Sister Teresa, the Principal, caught us.

Sister Teresa was a mean nun who never smiled. Her plump, aged face was pale white with orange freckles and overcast green eyes.

We knew we were on shit-street when we heard her knuckles pound the wired glass of the playground door. Her finger wagged furiously at us, perfectly synchronized to her frenzied lips. We couldn't hear a word she said and begged she'd disappear into a different nightmare. Instead, she pounded the glass harder still, eventually beckoning us in with her wicked index finger. She opened the door and howled.

"What on earth do you think you're doing up here?"

Her chubby, withered, translucent hands were open, looking like the Virgin Mary's great-grandmother. They showed off each and every greyish blue vein pumping holy blood to her burned-out heart. We had no reply, only nervous snickers.

"Jean-Pierre, you should know better. Now go to my office. Immediately! All three of you."

From her office, she gave us a stern warning, towering over us with her arms crossed, hands hidden in the sleeves of her dark blue habit.

"Well, what have you to say for yourselves?"

"Sorry, Sister Teresa. It won't happen again," replied Jean-Pierre.

"Next time, my punishment will be more severe. It will be the cane on your posteriors. Am I clear?"

"Yes, Sister Teresa," we said in unison and walked away fighting back our giggles.

"I'm not quite done with you yet, gentlemen."

She sent us to confession to ask the priest for forgiveness.

"Off with you!"

Though I didn't much care for confession, it was definitely a better option than the cane. I considered this a blessed day.

Religion confused me, though. If I did something wrong, I simply went to confession, and then it was all even-steven. Sounded like a free pass to me. I couldn't wait to be an adult and benefit from religious policies, as strange as they seemed. I wondered if God loved nuns and priests more than the rest of us.

Thank God, not all the teachers wore habits and mean expressions. My favorite teacher was Mrs. Matheson. None of the nuns were as kind or as beautiful as she. Mrs. Matheson always gave me lots of care and affection.

"Teacher's pet, teacher's pet," taunted some pupils. I didn't understand why. I never ever brought her a single apple. *I think they're jealous. They wouldn't be envious, whatsoever, if they knew what life was like at home. I wish I were like them. They have a Mum, a Dad, and food at home.*

It's probably just as well Mum rarely picked me up. The nuns frowned at her when she did. *She pongs of alcohol.* I hated the smell. I guess it's better to feel abandoned and lonely and watch the other kids kiss and hug their Mums and Dads rather than deal with the embarrassment of an alcoholic mother.

The next morning, the nuns made us pray as always. They reminded me Jesus loved me.

I think Mum loves me, too, in her own mysterious way, but I wonder sometimes. I don't think Dad does.

We never talked about our father at home, but he crossed my thoughts every now and again.

Jean-Pierre says the police sent Dad back home to Belgium and that his crimes were all too much for Mum to handle. She never recovered from what he did. I often asked.

"What did Dad get arrested for, Jean-Pierre?"

"Never you mind. You're too young."

"C'mon, tell me, man. I'm old enough. Where is he?"

"When you're older," he replied.

"Rudy, what happened to Dad?"

"Nothing, *Tonton,* don't worry about it. Like Jean-Pierre said, you're too young to understand."

"I'm not a kid anymore. I'm almost seven and can tie my own shoelaces."

No matter how much I insisted, the answers were always the same.

It must be really bad. Poor Mum.

It would be years before I discovered, let alone understood, the severity of his crimes.

Mum deteriorated after the New Year and always stayed sloshed, sad, and angry. She kicked us out of the flat regularly onto the cold winter streets during her drunken outbursts of frustration. Fortunately, we knew how to get back into the house through a narrow rear window that opened no more than a few inches. I squeezed through the constricted opening and let my brothers in through the front door. We snuck upstairs, past our flat, making use of the second floor landing for shelter. The three of us huddled and tried to sleep, fighting the cold. It made for an uncomfortable night, but at least we were inside.

Rudy's thick lips were blue and his teeth chattered. I couldn't feel my toes or my fingertips. My teeth prattled, too, and my nose ran.

Jean-Pierre's reassuring words formed mist in the night air.

"It will only be a bit longer. Imagine you're warm."

"I'm too cold to imagine anything," Rudy responded with a hint of anger in his voice.

"How do you know if you don't try?"

"I'm trying Jean-Pierre, but it's not working," I added.

"It takes time. Don't give up. Use willpower."

"You and your willpower," Rudy replied.

"Just be quiet and give it a try. Now huddle up and breathe deep and slow. We're gonna be fine, trust me. Willpower, it can make you do anything you want."

"Anything?" I asked.

"Yes. Starting from now you're gonna feel warm."

We eventually fell asleep, subdued by the rhythm of our own trembling. Maybe, there was some truth in this willpower stuff.

Later on our neighbor arrived home and witnessed us shivering in the corner.

"What on earf!" She said. You'll catch your deaf eh cold."

She invited us in to her flat and served us hot Ovaltine and asked a lot of questions. She had a nice TV and a nifty record player with big speakers. Pillows and a warm white duvet covered her comfortable bed. Inevitably, a pillow fight broke out. Rudy got a bit rough and almost knocked me out. I cried.

The neighbor held me tight with my head pressed against her chest and comforted me. Her breasts were big and soft. They felt good.

"I af to call the police, Jean-Pierre," our neighbor said.

"No, please." Jean-Pierre begged. "Mum's just not well right now. Things will be back to normal tomorrow."

"This can't appen again tomorrow."

"We know. But please, no police."

There was a pause. Jean-Pierre told Rudy and me that it was time to go home, before adding a final word to the neighbor.

"Thanks," he said. "I'm sure Mum's better already anyway."

We headed toward the door. Our neighbor followed us.

"Ang on, not so quickly," she said. "I fink I need to talk to your mum."

"It will only make it worse," replied Jean-Pierre. "You don't know our mum."

"Well then, I fink it's time I gots to know er, don't ya fink?"

She escorted us downstairs and knocked at Mum's door.

"Oh, there they are. I was worried," Mum said genuinely, looking at us then the neighbor. "Thank you. I didn't know what happened to them. I was so worried. *Tonton* darling, are you okay?"

Mum caressed my face. Her speech was slow and soft. Her eyes sat on the verge of tears.

"I don't means to be rude, Mrs. Jacob," said our neighbor, "but what were they doin' sleepin' on me landin', catchin' their deaf eh cold?"

"I beg your pardon."

"I'm just concerned, as I'm sure you are, Mrs. Jacob, about your kids. I didn't means to pry or sound rude."

"We're fine, thank you."

"Let me know if I can be of any elp."

"Good night."

"Wait--."

The door closed, ending the conversation. Mum cared for a few moments but soon regressed to anger.

"How can you do that to your mum?" She said to Jean-Pierre. "You humiliated me. That lady has no business getting into our affairs. How dare you? I carried you in my belly for nine months, suffered during labor for you. I sacrificed everything I owned in The Congo for you. And this is how you thank me? Shame on you!"

"But, Mum, I'm not even--."

"Don't you dare *but* me. I'm your mum, and you *will* listen to me and do as I say."

My elder brother remained silent.

Mum continued. "When I was your age I had to take care of my family. I had to walk over five miles to get water from a well."

"So you've told us."

"Get out. You just have to treat me with respect, and you can't even do that. Now get out. Don't come back until you have found your manners, Jean-Pierre Jacob. Leave!"

We followed Jean-Pierre instinctually and found ourselves back on the streets without our winter coats or scarves. It was freezing. I wished I'd grabbed my gloves. I had on a wooly jumper to keep me warm, which was more than my brothers. They only wore a shirt.

Jean-Pierre decided it best we not return to the neighbor, fearing the police, so we walked and walked all night until morning, sometimes running on the spot to warm up, but always on the lookout for a cop car. The last thing we wanted was for the police to see us. When the subzero temperature penetrated our bones, doorways made for emergency shelter. We couldn't even talk because our mouths lacked sensation.

Mum would have, hopefully, forgotten what happened by sunrise, and things would be back to normal.

The next morning, things were indeed back to "normal." Mum didn't remember a thing and sent us off to school from her bed, hung-over.

A week later, we were back on the landing huddled in the corner until the neighbor got home.

"I'm callin' the police this time, and telling the authorities in the morning."

"Please, we're fine. We don't want anybody to know about our situation. We've heard about kids who live in institutions," argued Jean-Pierre.

The neighbor picked me up and held me tight.

"Mum promised she was gonna' stop drinking and get better," Jean-Pierre continued.

The next couple of weeks were better as promised.

There was no alcohol at home. There was hope.

One evening, Mum got out of bed, even cooked us dinner, and was all dolled-up in a mini skirt and silver high heel shoes. She had make-up on and looked beautiful and smelled good. I was proud to have a beautiful Mum.

"I'm going to work," she said.

But before she could make it to the door, blood ran down her inner thigh, staining her panty hose. She collapsed. Jean-Pierre called the ambulance, and she was rushed to the hospital. We sat and waited at home. Nobody was hungry anymore. Dinner went to waste despite saying grace.

I began to have reservations about God, nuns and priests. None of them cared or listened.

CHAPTER 9

The remainder of the year flew by in a haze. Spring blossomed, the summer holidays came and went, and we became responsible for Mum since her hospital incident. I still didn't understand why any of this was happening to me, to us, to Mum. I didn't know what was wrong with her, only that she flailed in the wind like a dying autumn leaf. Winter loomed on the horizon.

Rent remained unpaid, so we moved yet again to a furnished place a mile away on Wright's Lane, around the corner from Kensington High Street Tube Station. It wasn't even a flat, but rather two separate rooms with a common landing on the first floor. Though much smaller, it was reasonably clean and rat free. Worse yet, Mum had no appetite and had lost considerable weight. Her health was deteriorating, and she didn't know her left from her right.

Mum's room was narrow with a bland single bed. To the right, by the sink in the corner, hung a meter that provided an hour of electricity per shilling.

All I remembered about our bedroom, which also acted as the living area, was how crowded and cramped it felt-- boxes in that corner, suitcases in this corner, an armoire here, two single beds there, and an armchair and a Chester drawer took up the remainder of space. Next door was a small toilet and bathtub we shared with our neighbors. It had a tiny window that couldn't open more than an inch. The room smelled damp and unhealthy. A broken mirror reflected the dim light. Hidden away under the vanity cabinet waited another meter. This one swallowed shillings by the minute, and not the hour like the other one by our bare fridge in Mum's room. She hadn't worked in months, so we had no extra shillings for a hot bath.

Food came courtesy of a small side window from the restaurant below. She had befriended the cook. The man had dark greasy hair parted to one side. His thick and foreign accent labored for words. I didn't like him. He eyed Mum in ways I didn't understand but evoked uneasiness.

I hated it when I came home from school to find him in our flat drinking with her. The place sniffed peculiar. The unmade bed aroused my suspicion. Mum's nighty seemed inappropriate.

In the evening, Mum would send me down the outside fire escape to the restaurant window. The greasy cook prepared a bowl of big, fat, juicy French fries and sautéed vegetables. That Christmas Eve he even served us a thick piece of roast ham on a platter. I thanked him, of course, and wished him a Merry Christmas. He rubbed my head as a gesture of friendship.

"Don't touch my hair, man! Nobody's allowed to touch my hair."

On weekends, Mum took me on shoplifting sprees to high-street retail chains like Woolworth's and Marks and Spencer. She stuffed clothes up her fur coat, looking pregnant. The clothes were usually for my brothers and me, but she sometimes spoiled herself, too. I guess she didn't want anybody to know we were poor.

We stole until one time we got caught.

A few stashed items fell from her coat onto the floor in the middle of an aisle. Someone had to have seen.

"Mum, Mum, you dropped these."

She hurried away.

"Mum. What about these? Wait for me, Mum!"

We got caught. Security escorted us through the store to an office in the back. It was small, boring beige, and smoky. They took Mum elsewhere, leaving me alone for a long time to sit in horror.

Will she go to jail like Dad? Am I going to be taken away?

I was tempted to cry but held back my tears, knowing Mum would be proud of me if I remained strong. I wanted her to be proud of me.

A heavy man with a thick mustache entered the tiny office. The top button of his shirt was undone with a stain on the chest. He had forgotten to fasten the top button of his stained shirt.

I would never wear a tie with an unbuttoned shirt. Mum taught me better than that.

He questioned me from behind his desk.

I don't know, was my consistent response to all his questions. That and, *I want my mum.*

"In a while lad," he answered.

"Where's my mum?"

"We'll get to that in a minute, young man. I need you to sit still. I shall be back momentarily."

He left the office, closing the door behind him, taking all the oxygen. The walls constricted. I suffocated with fright. The frames on the wall ogled me. Every faint sound magnified. I sat, stared at the floor and worried.

My legs couldn't reach the floor, so I swung them back and forth to keep calm. My clammy, blood-starved palms were firmly tucked between the upholstered chair and my thighs.

We're going to jail. I just know it. It's my fault.

Eternity seemed to pass by before a very tall lady entered. She talked to me softly, crouching to offer me a soda.

"No, thank you," I replied.

"What a well-mannered young man you are. How old are you, Vital?" the lady asked.

I ignored the question.

She continued unabashed, "Cat got your tongue, has it? Just so you know, I'm on your side. That man wasn't very friendly, was he?"

I chuckled. She offered me candy.

"No, thank you," I said. "I don't eat sweets. They're bad for your teeth."

"Indeed they are. So how old did you say you are Vital?"

"I don't know."

"Of course you do. Don't be silly. Let me guess. I think you must be about five."

"I'm seven-and-a-half!" I crossed my arms, huffed, and sulked. *Why does everybody think I'm only five when I'm almost seven-and-three-quarters? I'm such a half pint. I hate it. I wish my feet could touch the floor.*

She asked a lot more questions, most unrelated to shoplifting.

Apparently satisfied with her interrogation, the tall, kind lady exited the office, leaving the door ajar. I heard voices in the hallway. Somebody closed the door, probably realizing I was listening. The voices turned to mumbles. Then, all went quiet. The silence deafened my ears. Each tock became a shudder, each tic a blow. I swung my legs faster.

A knock at the door perforated the suffocating stillness. The heavy gentleman with the stain on his shirt reentered. I wanted to strangle him with his undone tie, demanding Mum's release and my freedom. Instead, my pulse tripled and I froze with fear.

I am going to jail.

"Stand up, young man," he said, beckoning me with his hand. I jumped down and waited for his next order. "Come on."

He opened the door, pushing me in the middle of my back to pass under his arm and out the door. Mum waited in the hallway. She extended her arm, grabbed my hand, and walked down the hallway in haste, back into the store, and straight outside.

What a lucky day. We didn't go to jail.

"Mum, I'm sorry," I whispered. "I'm sorry, Mum."

She said nothing. I felt horrible. It was my fault that we got caught. I planned to make it up to her.

The next day, I stole a ring from a different Woolworth's confident she would love it and be proud of me. The golden ring had a light purple diamond on it and twinkled like a distant star.

"It's beautiful, *Tonton*," she said from her bed after I gave it to her.

"Where did you get it?"

I hesitated.

"*Tonton*?" She repeated with a frown that suggested I should be careful.

"I got it from Woolworth's down the street."

"How much was it?"

I realized she would not approve and that what I did was wrong, but it was too late. I gawked at the floor to avoid the question.

"*Tonton!*"

"It didn't cost anything, Mum. I took it without paying."

"You stole it."

"Um, yes."

"You know that's wrong. Go get my belt."

"I'm sorry, Mum. Please don't--".

"Ah, ah! Go get my belt."

She taught me a lesson I would never forget. My backside burned like a wild fire. I screamed for mercy like a tortured heretic at the stake.

"Stop crying or stand in the corner," she told me.

I hated the corner and tried really hard to stop crying. I failed.

"Vital Maximilien Germain Jacob, get in the corner. Now!"

As I walked to the corner against my will, attempting to sneak in the odd plea for mercy, she continued to hit me with her hands. I shrieked even louder than before.

"Stop, please. Mum, please."

The more I screeched and attempted to negotiate, the more she hit. The more she hit, the more I bargained. I felt slaps on my backside, my thighs, and my hands that were desperate to protect me.

I reached the corner, sobbing and whimpering, praying to God for salvation and safeguard. He answered my prayers. A first. The slaps stopped. I sniffled, shuddered, and sweltered from the pain, turning around to get her attention. She ignored me.

When my brothers came home, they got a walloping, too. Jean-Pierre received the worst of it. She blamed him for my actions. I felt guilty. Rudy let his tears fly. Jean-Pierre stayed emotionless. He didn't seem to feel the pain, which angered Mum even more. She lashed harder with her belt.

"Please, Mum, you're hurting him," I pleaded. "He didn't do anything."

"Stop! Please," begged Rudy, grabbing her arm.

In due time, the anguish ended. All three of us faced separate corners in silence on our knees until she forgave and lectured us.

"Jean-Pierre, you are responsible for your little brother. It's your job to guide and protect him," Mum said. "Understood?"

He nodded.

"You, too, Rudy." She paused. "*Tonton*, I am proud of you. It takes courage to tell the truth. You will be a good man one day. Don't ever forget today's lesson."

"Yes, Mum."

"Never steal again, okay, *cheri*."

"*Oui, Maman*."

"As for you Jean-Pierre, shame on you for not supervising your little brother."

"What did I do? I was at school," Jean-Pierre said.

"Don't talk back! Listen to me! Stealing is an act of cowards. I didn't raise cowards. An honorable man must earn his living. He must earn respect and work for possessions. Life is not easy and is full of difficult choices. Always try to make the best choice with what you have. Commit to life, to each other. Be true to yourselves and your dreams. Dream big and let nothing hold you back. Nothing."

Her words touched me, but the situation left me confused and unable to sit, because my bum still burnt.

How can she steal and be the almighty hand of God at the same time?

"I forgive you, *Tonton*. You, too, Jean-Pierre. Rudy, always be there for your brothers."

Mum held me close, kissed me, and smiled. Her big beautiful white smile shone like the sun, bright and full of warmth. My sniffling turned to giggles as she tickled my stomach. She clutched a hanky from her sleeve and smothered my face in it, telling me to blow. I blew a stream of snot that made me laugh. Rudy laughed, also. The snot went everywhere, including back up my nose. I giggled some more.

Mum returned to her room and her booze, leaving us to ourselves. That's the angriest she had ever been and the hardest she'd ever hit Jean-Pierre. I couldn't help but ask if he was okay. I loved my brother so much I would have taken every belt lash in his place.

"Yeah, of course, I'm okay," he replied in his customary cool demeanor. "It tingled a bit, that's all. Besides, she didn't mean it."

"Are we ever gonna get back to how things were before?"

"Of course, *Tonton*. Of course."

He rubbed my head. I leaned away and fixed my hair.

"Watch my hair, man," I announced.

The next day, Mum made me return the ring.

At the store entrance, I begged her to not make me go in there, promising I would never steal again. The walk was long. Climbing Everest would have been easier. Everybody in the store stared at me.

They must know I'm a criminal.

We arrived at the counter and Mum called the lady over. She had small golden glasses with a double lens on the bridge of her narrow nose.

"Yes, madam. How can I be of assistance," she asked Mum.

"This young boy has something to say and give back," Mum answered.

The lady took off her glasses and let them hang from the gold chain that wrapped around her very wrinkled neck. She lowered her chin and fixed her eyes on me. I said nothing.

She raised her eyebrows and observed Mum.

"Well, Vital," Mum said. "Don't you have a confession to make?"

I had never felt so embarrassed in my life. I wanted to hide in the priest's confession chamber until the Virgin Mary herself appeared to hear my confession instead of this stranger staring at me.

With my eyes glued to the floor, I pulled the ring from out of my pocket and mumbled an apology.

"I beg your pardon," the woman said. "I couldn't hear you."

"Speak up Vital, and what did I tell you? Look at adults in the eye when addressing them. Say what you need to say."

I looked up but couldn't bear to see the lady's face and gazed off to the side, swaying my body from side to side.

"I came to say sorry for stealing this ring and I want to give it back because it's wrong to steal…and I'm sorry for stealing."

I burst into tears and gripped Mum's leg to hide my face.

The lady walked around the counter and crouched next to me. "Well, let me see the ring."

I extended my hand without looking until she took it.

"Now, I hope you've learned a lesson from this, young man," she said. "Next time, we might have to call the police and send you to jail. Do you want to go to jail?

"No."

Mum apologized and we exited the store. I promised myself I would never ever steal again. When would all these lessons end?

CHAPTER 10

After a brief period of stability and another long winter, Mum rolled back down to the bottom of the hill with even greater speed, landing with a thick splat into the mud. We spent more nights kicked out on the streets. Even Jean-Pierre, who once defended her so severely, finally decided enough was enough and took us to a police station around the corner on Earls Court Road to report her.

They ignored his plea, telling us to go home.

Home?

I pounded the door to our flat.

"Mum, can we come back in. Mum! It's cold. Mum!"

My pleas fell on deaf ears.

"Stop it, Vital, she's probably passed out," Jean-Pierre advised me.

Our friendly neighbor wasn't there to take us in anymore, either. Instead, we spent the night in a hostel in Holland Park. Jean-Pierre's strength and wisdom got us through. The next day, we went to school full of smiles as if nothing had happened.

Though sad, my smile remained sincere yet ugly with its very crooked teeth. My lower front teeth lived underneath the base of my tongue and stood at right angles to each other. I hated my teeth. I also hated the tooth fairy. She never ever left me as much as a single shilling, let alone a penny under my pillow.

I peered into the broken mirror in the bathroom and saw an unhappy little clown. Happiness was apparently a hiccup in life.

Jean-Pierre's repeated promise said that Mum would get better one day and that all would be well, if we willed it. His ice-cold optimism was contagious. I actually believed in tomorrow. Yet, after further nights on the streets and a couple more visits to the police station, the officers finally took my big brother seriously and escorted us home in a police car.

A policewoman talked to Mum. Within minutes, they left. A strange stillness filled the flat.

We returned to the station the next day. Life took a drastic left turn. Just the night before we had walked the streets; the next day we were seated in a courtroom with the support of a young female social worker.

The courtroom felt intimidating and quiet. It reminded me of church. I sat next to Mum. My brothers sat with the social worker on another bench.

The judge had thinning white hair. The bridge of his nose supported sleek silver spectacles that flickered in the light as he moved his head up and down in observation of the proceedings. He questioned Mum first, then the social worker and, finally, Jean-Pierre and Rudy. Both of my brothers related how bad our mother was and how much she'd neglected us.

I witnessed anger, and revenge maybe in Jean-Pierre's eyes. Rudy's simply looked sad.

Their words evoked such powerful emotions. I cringed. I hated Mum for all she hadn't done, yet I loved her with all my heart, too. She was my Mum.

How dare they condemn her?

But I loved them. Love, hate—I didn't know which was which anymore.

After deep thought, the judge stared and asked if anybody had anything to add. I raised my arm.

"Stand up, young man," he said. "You must be, ah, of course, you must be Mr. Vital Jacob."

I nodded, my hands hidden beneath my thighs while I swung my legs. Mum pushed me gently to stand up.

"Tell the truth," she whispered.

I smiled, ready to address the court. My mouth opened, but no words came.

"Well, young man, what have you to add?"

I took a deep breath and raised my right hand, palm facing the judge like a cub scout taking an oath.

"Your Honor, everything, everything that, umm--."

"Don't be afraid, Mr. Jacob," said the judge. "Speak up like a brave young man."

There was a moment of silence. I hesitated.

Though his voice was warm and he seemed kind, fear consumed me. I glanced at Mum, then across to my brothers and the social worker, then back at Mum. She closed her eyes and nodded as if to say it's okay.

"Your Honor," I said. "Everything my brothers told the court is the truth, the whole truth and nothing but the truth, so help me God."

Mum grimaced. I felt both proud and ashamed—proud because I had addressed the court like a young man with courage, ashamed because I had just vended my mother to the court for less than Judas sold Jesus to the High Priest, Caiaphas. I didn't even honor her with a kiss before inserting my betrayal.

The judge ruled our mother unfit to take care of her three children. He committed us into an institution, or a home, as it was ironically called.

I should have kept quiet. Again, it was my entire fault. Why didn't I simply keep my mouth shut? Now I'm an orphan. A sad, lonely clown without a smile.

The institution, my new home, was in a dangerous rundown neighborhood of West London called Ladbroke Grove, not far from Notting Hill Gate, famous for it's Caribbean Carnival. The name of the street and the home was Oxford Gardens. Around the corner and beneath the flyover sat a famous market on Portobello Road decorated with badly executed graffiti, plenty of litter, and the stench of ripe urine. I was not yet nine.

The building's façade was a flinty blue. It did not blend into the residential environment. The structure's interior emitted a flavorless pragmatic vibe deprived of love and a soul. It smelled of loss and sorrow, like a hospital ward for the terminally ill. The kids were divided onto two separate floors by age. My brothers resided on the second, leaving me alone on the first.

Gray linoleum flooring ran the length of the hallways, overlapping into bedrooms filled with iron beds that looked borrowed from an army barracks. The sterile living room contained only a black and white TV to add color. The torn, worn-out furniture was uncomfortable.

My bedroom had four small single beds with rigid white sheets and pallid blankets. I shared it with two Black boys my age and one older Caucasian boy who called us coons. The honky boy, as we called him back, was mean and made us do things we didn't like. Most best forgotten and not talked about.

The dining area was row after row of meek tables with ugly chairs. The kitchen staff was as sweet as boiled cabbage with corned beef. The breakfast porridge tasted so bad and salty we never asked for more. I did enjoy the custard and apple crumble though but, of dessert, we were never allowed seconds.

We all ate together as one dejected dysfunctional non-family. If the quality of the food illustrated the worst of British cooking, then the arguments, overturned tables, and recurring fistfights definitely added spice and punch. It was basically a nuthouse for kids with little chance of deliverance. We were simply a statistic waiting to happen. We'd inevitably become damaged bastards, social misfits or cynical menaces confined to handcuffs, bars, and chains.

We were all so different from each other, yet the almighty hand of rejection unified us like super glue. It was but a matter of time before we would get arrested or caught up in drugs or other crimes.

I intended to overcome this temporary insanity someway, somehow. At least, I hoped I could. Hope is all I had other than Jean-Pierre and Rudy. But hope was one thing. Reality was another. The idea of a cop dragging me out in handcuffs with a knife in my gut or foam streaming from my mouth due to an overdose was not what I had planned for my future.

I couldn't decide if living in a "home" filled with juvenile delinquents, pubescent drug users and under-aged prostitutes was better or worse than living dirt poor with an alcoholic mother.

During the first weeks, I underwent endless psychological evaluations: tests, questions, and more examinations followed by interviews. The authorities came to their conclusions. I came to mine. This home was not a home, as they called it. It was a prison sentence.

After two months, the authorities moved us to another institution. This new home was nice. It was made up of two big, beautiful three-story houses on a quiet suburban street named Howard's Lane in a neighborhood in South West London called Putney. The houses were customized to accommodate their purpose, to mask the institution.

One house served for the girls; the other, for the boys. Though not as tragic as the last place, this institution still had one or two odd jobs with a few missing nuts.

About eight children lived here, plus a dog named Hardy. Hardy was a savvy street mutt that looked like a cross between an Irish Setter and a fox. He did as he pleased, including roaming the streets at will to make friends and trouble, a common trend at the home.

The wardens of the house were an elderly married couple named Bob and Ena. They invited us to address them, and all other staff members, as uncle and auntie. It seemed strange at first, but I liked the idea even though they weren't genuine family. It made for a warmer environment than the previous place.

I quickly became friends with a young boy named Mark Tracy. Like everybody else, including the staff, but other than my brothers and me, he was white.

Mark looked typical Irish, with long dark strawberry blonde hair, translucent white skin, freckles, and skinny, knobby knees. He wore standard thick-rimmed black glasses provided for free by the National Health. They were not very flattering, and the other kids mocked him.

He called me V for short. I liked that nickname and adopted it. The name *Tonton* was buried.

I would, however, still let Mum use it if, and when, I ever saw her again.

Everybody called Jean-Pierre *John*-Pierre, because they couldn't pronounce the French *Jean*. The John part sounded funny, and I teased him about it, sometimes calling him just John whenever angry. He didn't like it. Eventually he became simply JP for short.

Mark Tracy had lived in this home for a while with his elder sister, Alison. Alison was very pretty and nice to me. I fancied her and acted shy whenever she strolled close.

"We were the first to move into this new home," Alison explained.

"Yes, and it's not our only home," Mark continued. "We've been in and out of several. This is the best one, so far."

"How comes you ended up here?" I asked.

"Our parents got a divorce. Neither of them wanted to take care of us," Alison said. "We don't need them anyway. We're doin' just fine, the two of us."

At least Mum didn't abandon me, I thought, but didn't say.

Mark and I shared a room on the first floor with Rudy. JP had his own room up in the attic, because he was the second oldest after a boy named Tom. Tom occupied the larger of the two lofts. I loved the attic and hoped to move up there when older, if I wasn't yet living with Mum again.

Tom was sixteen, a longhaired lout with a mean attitude and a bully. I'd heard the staff refer to him as a problem kid. I wished JP would knock his teeth out.

"What good would that do?" JP responded.

"Cause he's always picking on everyone when you're not around and he's a prick, that's why," I said.

"Don't worry V. He knows not to touch you."

"Yeah, but still...what about the others?"

"I don't work here. That's the staff's job."

"Just punch him to Timbuktu, anyway. He deserves a good knuckle sandwich."

JP explained that avoiding aggression was better than confrontation. That's what he learned from years of Kung Fu classes, he told me. I hated it when he talked like a wise ass.

"Yeah, well, from what I remember, you weren't exactly sir non-aggression that one New Year's Eve, Mr. Moped-attacking-army-belt-swinging-Kung-Fu-master-and-a-half."

JP scowled. "Don't be a wise ars, V."

"Oh, shut-up, John. Stop acting like a fuddy-duddy. Wise ars this!"

I punched him in his belly and ran away laughing. His stomach was solid. It hurt my hand, but I was all smiles and legs.

"I got ya, JP." He chased. "I got ya."

He caught me and put me in a body lock until I said sorry.

"Sorry for what?" I shouted. "Let me go! You're hurting me, John.

"My name is Jean-Pierre, not John. Now, say sorry, *Tonton*."

"My name's not *Tonton*. It's Vital. But you can call me V."

"Who's gonna make me, *Tonton*."

"Whatever, John. Now let go of me, I need to use the john, John."

"Whatever, *Tonton.*"

I played stubborn, preferring to cry rather than apologize.

"You're breaking my arm, you bully."

I yelled for help. He let go. I whined and walked away.

"I still got ya, so there," I said. "Just wait till you're old and decrepit, JP. Then you'll be beggin' me for mercy, man."

We had lots of play fights. Problem was, I always lost and got hurt. I would've been better off playing with cars. Football, even. At least, I could win at that against him.

My new friend Mark had a car collection. Mine was left behind with everything else due to all the sudden moving.

Our bedroom was quite big. It had three single beds, one for me, one for Mark and one for Rudy. We each had our own set of generic drawers and closet. There was a very clean, snowy porcelain sink in the corner by the white framed bay windows. They overlooked the front garden, filled with roses, trees, and other beautiful plants and flowers. Though it scared me at night, my favorite was the Monkey Puzzle Tree that stared into the bedroom. I could see hidden faces in its branches.

I kept my fear a secret, as I did every other emotion that plagued me, including abandonment. I realized I didn't have a safety net. If I fell, it would hurt. Nobody would kiss the wound better. JP might punch whoever pushed me down or hurt me, but he didn't do kisses.

Two boys occupied the room further down the landing. I forget their names. At the end of the landing sat two toilets and a bathroom. They were warm and dry, and didn't have a meter. Hot water was free and plentiful. I supposed some things were better in a "home."

A passageway next to the bathrooms connected the two houses. It was off limits. The staff kept us well separated from the girls. Just as well, because I didn't like girls, although Alison was an exception.

The dining room had nice square tables that seated four, making it somewhat pleasant. We actually had salt and pepper shakers like in restaurants.

Breakfast was at 7:00 a.m., supper at 5:30 p.m. They served lunch at 12:30 p.m., precisely, without forgiveness.

Mildred, the cook, was very old, with white hair and ever so sweet, but she always burned things.

"Bloody ell, Mildred, I can cook better than this," Tom would complain.

"Mind your manners, young man," Mildred would answer back. "A little singe never hurt anybody. When I was your age, we were grateful for our rations. Now, eat up, you ungrateful little so and so."

"A little singe? I've eaten coal that tasted better than this bollocks."

"Watch your mouth, Tom! Now apologize," Uncle Derrick demanded.

The conversation escalated. Tom got punished. No dessert. He was forced to sit, wait, and watch us eat sponge pudding and custard.

After supper, we all cleared our own tables and took turns doing dishes. Tonight it's the boys' turn. One washed the pink plastic dishes, Tom rinsed against his will, two dried, and one put them away.

The living room had a sturdy, dark green carpet made up of individual squares that could be alternated at will. Against the back wall rested a thick-textured orange couch. An identical brown one sat perpendicular a few feet away. The added beanbag chairs and armchairs allowed us all to watch TV together. A colored TV.

Two large, white French doors opened to the rear garden, which was filled with an abundance of fruit trees and bushes. A huge weeping willow lived in the corner, shading half the garden.

Once, the home's gardener told me and Mark in his thick Yorkshire accent, "That there tree is over one thousand years old, lads. Planted by the Druids, it were. If you hug it, you can feel its soul and hear its stories."

"Really?" I asked only half convinced.

"Aye."

We hugged the tree. There was nothing to feel or hear.

"Crazy old gardener," I mumbled as he left.

To the right of the tree sat cages for the guinea pigs and a rabbit. I loved feeding the rabbit carrots and lettuce, but needed to be careful to not lose a finger when its dicers nipped away. He was a plump thing, yet springy, with a thick black and white coat, very big ears, long whiskers, and a little pink nose that was always on the sniff.

The last time Mark and I played with the rabbit in its run, he escaped. The gardener snitched to uncle Bob, who got mad.

"Didn't I warn you to be careful, boys?" Bob said.

We both trembled and promised it would never happen again. He docked our pocket money for the week.

To the right of the willow rested a dark, old shed filled with spider webs, corroded tools, discarded bike frames, and spare parts.

Inside, a bright yellow chopper caught Mark's and my eye, even though it was missing a front wheel, the double saddle, and chain. Instantly, we planned to rebuild it.

The week whizzed by. First thing Saturday morning, Mark and I were in the shed. We stole a wheel from one bike and a saddle from another. There wasn't one single working chain, however, to finish the task.

"Let's play with the rabbit instead," Mark suggested.

"No way. What if he escapes again?" I said.

"We'll be careful. Besides, Uncle Bob's gone."

After thirty minutes of bunny play in the run, we closed the trap door and headed back to the shed.

"All we need is a chain, for Pete's sake, Mark. How much can it cost?"

"A couple of quid, maybe. I've got some money saved up. What about you, V?"

"I can smash my piggy bank now instead of at Christmas."

We walked up to our room where I painstakingly wiggled the coins out of the piggy bank.

I sighed.

"Oh, well, there goes Christmas."

With Mark's savings and my small change, we had a couple of pounds.

"Let's ask Auntie Ena if we can go to the bike shop now."

"What about the rabbit?" I asked.

"Oh, no!"

"We're dead. Uncle Bob's gonna go bonkers," I tell Mark.

When we got back down to the garden, the rabbit had done a disappearing act.

"Crap! Where'd he go?" asked Mark.

"How am I supposed to bloody know?"

I took a moment and eyed around.

"Sneaky little bugger! There he is."

"Where?"

"Can't you see anything without your glasses?"

Mark huffed at my comment. I shrugged my shoulders and raised my eyebrows in regret.

"Look, look! He's right there at east northeast."

"I see him. Now what?"

I pulled a face.

"How did he escape, anyway?"

"How am I supposed to know? Now, shh," I begged.

I snuck into position. "He's running toward the willow. Cut him off."

"I can't see him."

"He's legging it back to the bushes."

"Where?"

"Shhh!"

I pointed. We stood still for a moment. Mark waited for my cue.

The rabbit wiggled his nose at us, winked, and then made another dash for it.

I yelled out, "Grab him!"

The rabbit doubled back and leapt my way.

"He's yours," Mark said.

I dove to the right. The bouncing bunny swerved left and slipped through my hands.

"Butter fingers," Mark said, laughing at my expense.

"Shut up, four-eyes. At least I can see him."

Twenty minutes later, the cheeky rabbit found himself trapped in the corner of the garden with nowhere to go. He appeared finally tired of toying with us. We pounced on him, ending the chase. We placed him back in his cage and let him know he'd been a bad bunny. Uncle Bob was none the wiser.

"You couldn't even catch a cold with those hands, V," Mark said.

"Shut up. Next time, we should play with the guinea pigs."

"They're easier to catch."

"Yeah, all they do is stuff their cheeks. They're boring and full of crap. Just like you, Mark."

He chased me through the garden until we were out of breath all over again.

Later, with permission from Auntie Ena, we hurried to the bike shop to buy our missing chain. The clerk told us we only needed the link and saved us a couple of shillings. On the way home, we spoiled ourselves with ice cream.

The link fit and our chopper worked. We argued over who got to ride first.

"Why don't we ride together," I said.

"Okay, but I'm the oldest, so I get to sit at the front first and steer. You peddle."

"Alright, but then we're changing."

"Agreed. Jump on!"

We cycled around the garden like stumbling idiots, but had a blast. To make it more fun and challenging, I stood on the back rack with no hands while he steered and peddled. Then we switched, and he sat on the handlebars.

The cook said we should join the circus.

How silly. The circus was for clowns and elephants. Surely, she should know that at her age.

CHAPTER 11

New kids arrived over the next few months. Many left in haste for varied reasons. I wished Tom would leave.

Uncle Derrick was my favorite staff member. He's about six-foot-five and well built, playful, kind and caring, allowing us all to sit on his lap, sometimes simultaneously, because he's so big. Not to mention he could sing like Elvis. Mum would have loved my new uncle just for his singing. He could get strict when needed, however, keeping us all in check. We both loved and feared him. Well, everybody except Tom.

One school day after supper, an argument between Tom and Uncle Derrick started in the kitchen. It didn't concern burnt food this time or the word bollocks. Tom was pissed off for no other reason than determination to stand up for his rights and what he called his "cause".

"I'm not doing dishes tonight, Derrick."

"First of all, it's *Uncle* Derrick. You're rinsing."

"I'll rinse when I bloody well feel like it. You can't make me, so get lost. I have rights."

Uncle Derrick wouldn't let him exit the kitchen and stood there like a brick wall. Tom tried to bulldoze his way out but bounced off our bouncer uncle, who pinned him down to the floor by twisting his arms behind his back.

Everybody in the home gathered in the kitchen and enjoyed the humiliation of our disliked bully, who was kissing the floor in apology. When he calmed down, Uncle

Derrick let him go. Tom wiped his nose on his forearm and disappeared. We all chanted Derrick's name like adoring soccer fans.

With the dishes done and Tom's "cause" ended, me and a few others played soccer in the backyard with Uncle Derrick. He's good, but I could hold my own and dribble circles around his long legs. Mark hated soccer and stayed inside.

Between the goal celebrations and the panting, came a commotion from the cutlery drawer in the kitchen. We couldn't see who or what through the big kitchen window that overlooked the back garden, but it was loud. The clanging didn't sound like the sweet old cook, but more like the mad Swedish chef in the Muppets having a disgruntled fit. The back door slammed. Tom stood there enraged, holding a dull ten-inch knife in his right hand.

"You're a dead man, Derrick," he said, removing strands of hair that stuck to his salivating mouth.

I had the urge to be cheeky and say, "First of all, it's Uncle Derrick," but the knife affected my ability to speak.

Something's gonna get cut, and it ain't gonna be me.

Ironically, Tom wouldn't cut his own hair, but he seemed prepared to slash Uncle Derrick's flesh to shreds like a barbaric barber.

With fury plastered all over his face, Tom yelled, "How dare you humiliate me like that?"

I rushed inside, barging through several doors into the hallway, yelling up the wooden bannisters to JP's room on the third floor. There was no response. I tried again.

"JP! Jean-Pierre!"

"What?"

"'Urry up. Tom's got a knife. He's gonna kill Derrick!"

"Come again, V," he responded, leaning over the banister to look down the staircase.

"'Urry up. Tom's gonna stab Uncle Derrick with a knife in the back garden."

As JP flew down the stairs one landing at a time, I rushed back outside. Tom had edged closer to Derrick, whose hands now hovered in front of him, fingers up, palms toward Tom.

"Easy, Tom. Let's talk about this."

"I don't want to talk, you fucking cunt."

"Listen, put down the knife before somebody gets hurt."

Tom stole a few inches. Uncle Derrick backed up, glanced behind him and realized he'd run out of space. Though trapped by the bushes, he remained composed.

"What good is this going to do, Tom?"

"Shut up!"

"Alright, but...."

"I said, shut up, 'Uncle' Derrick. Who the 'ell are you to tell me what I'm supposed to do?"

"Jean-Pierre's coming, Uncle Derrick," I stated.

"F-off, V, you little runt," replied Tom.

"I wasn't talking to you, Tom, so there."

"Stay out of this, V," interrupted Uncle Derrick, before telling us all to get inside.

Nobody moved. My blood pumped through my veins like pressurized break fluid. I've never seen anybody get stabbed before. Where's my big brother? He's coming, I reminded myself. Jean-Pierre wasn't on his way, he'd arrived, and grabbed Tom without a stutter.

I yelled, "Watch out."

Within seconds, all was said and done. My big brother disarmed Tom in a heroic split second of martial arts brilliance, saving Uncle Derrick from a scalping. Tom found himself once again kissing the ground with his arms twisted behind his back.

"You wankers!" he screeched.

"Who's the bully now, Tom?" I declared. "Got what you deserved, didn't ya, you bloody ippy. Get an 'air cut."

"Someone go and get Auntie Ena or Uncle Bob. Tell them to call the police," Uncle Derrick asked.

All the while, my brother's firm palm smothered one

side of Tom's face, pressing the other into the dried, worn-out grass.

"I'll fucking kill you, too, John," Tom spat out. "Let me go! I said, let me go!"

"Calm down or I'll break your arm."

"Arrghh!"

"I warned you, now calm down. Besides, my name is Jean-Pierre. If you're nice, I'll let you call me JP."

The police arrived and escorted Tom into a marked car. The cops drove him away cursing into the sunset, never to be seen again.

Uncle Derrick survived a scare and lived to sing *Blue Suede Shoes* another day. Thank you very much, JP. All in all, it was just another day in child care.

At least, no blood got spilled.

CHAPTER 12

Every six weeks or so, our assigned social worker paid a visit. Their job was to interact with us for about an hour, analyze us, talk and meet with staff members, file reports, and arrive at conclusions to determine our futures. They, too, like everybody else, came and went, changing like the seasons. There was, however, only one season in child care. Winter!

My current social worker's name was Claude Esposito. He had dark hair and a thick beard. I viewed him as the enemy, even though he pretended to care. Today was my visit.

Claude did not arrive alone. He entered the staff room with his committee, reinforced by Auntie Ena, Uncle Bob, and whoever was on duty that day. I waited around anxiously, knowing I would be called in later.

I wished Uncle Derrick were here. He was on our side.

"We're ready for you, Vital. Come on in."

"Thank you, Claude."

A large teapot brewed on the dresser, with milk and sugar on a tray. The biscuits lay on a dainty bone china side plate that we never used.

They all had a little teacup placed in front of them on a matching saucer atop the coffee table and side stands.

Claude's long legs were crossed. He wore a dark suit. His black briefcase sat open at the base of his armchair. I had never met the other committee members who held pens in hand, folders on laps, and profound expressions.

"Have a seat, Vital," Uncle Bob said.

"Would you like a cup of tea and some biscuits?" asked Auntie Ena.

I felt important and responded with enthusiasm.

"Yes, please."

What a privilege to drink from bone china cups and not from the "standard issue" dirty-pink plastic ones.

I watched the hot brew splash into the cup and emit steam.

"Two sugars, please."

"Help yourself to biscuits," Uncle Bob said, holding the assortment in front of me.

"They are splendid," added Auntie Ena.

I crossed my legs, attempting to behave like a grown-up. Who were these additional people, and why were they here? I prepared myself for my Spanish Inquisition.

"How is everything, Vital?" inquired Claude, politely.

"Fine."

"I've brought some people from the head office who are here to talk about some very promising things that we are excited to share with you."

I smiled and sipped further from my tea, nibbling away at my favorite milk chocolate McVities biscuit. They tasted even better when dipped in tea, but I refrained from dipping to make a good impression.

Claude went through the formalities of introducing me to each of his colleagues. He began the conversation.

"We see your school grades are excellent, and your form teacher, Miss Eaton, speaks highly of you. Do you like your new school?"

"Yes, I do. Miss Eaton's my favorite teacher."

"We consider you a very intelligent and talented boy, and Auntie Ena tells me you like to play piano with Helen."

Helen was a girl at the home of the same age and very good on piano. She taught me how to play chopsticks and the basics of Beethoven's *Fur Elise*. I loved the piano.

"What do you think about piano lessons? Would you like that?" asked one committee member.

"That would be wonderful, thank you."

"Fantastic. We'll look into starting you with Helen's teacher."

That was indeed exciting news, but they didn't need a committee to ask me that.

"How are you getting along with the other kids?" asked another committee member.

"Well, I'm good friends with Mark Tracy and get along with everybody else, pretty much."

Claude resumed the questions with a weighty expression hiding behind his beard and thick eyebrows.

"We've analyzed your file very carefully, Vital, and have taken everything into consideration, how you came into care, your parents' history and your brothers, who we know you love dearly."

He paused, sipped from his cup, glanced at his allies, and continued.

"We think a foster family would be wonderful for you."

The question threw me aback.

"I don't understand."

"What would you think of joining a foster family?"

"Why would I need a foster family?"

Another member intervened.

"Well, we are convinced that a foster family would be the best thing for you. It would provide you with everything you need for a stable future."

"What about Jean-Pierre and Rudy?" I asked.

"We'll find a beautiful family for each one of you," responded Claude.

"So you want to split us up?"

Nobody offered an immediate answer, and an awkward silence lingered in the air. Claude broke the stillness.

"Well, I wouldn't put it that way. What we really want is, you see, we thought that, I guess we all simply want what's best for you, Vital. You're a wonderful young man with such a promising future, and the structure of a home is limiting."

Another member backed up Claude's hesitant statement.

"All kids are afraid at first, but all of them end up very happy with their foster parents. We understand you're afraid and it's normal."

I was fully aware that all these educated people assessing me neither knew me nor understood me, yet they plotted to determine my future like a pawn in a chess game. Of course, they didn't understand. They were not me. They had never worn my shoes. I wanted to tell them to piss off and shove their ideas up their backsides. I wished I had balls like Tom and could make a stand for my "cause." I remained polite and meek.

"Can I talk to my brothers about this?"

"We've already spoken to Jean-Pierre."

"It's JP. We don't call him Jean-Pierre anymore."

"Very well then. JP loves you very much and wants what's best for you, too. He wants you to be happy."

"I am happy. I like it here. I don't need another family. I have JP and Rudy to take care of me."

"Yes, but Jean-Pierre."

"It's JP!"

"I mean, JP, will be old enough to leave soon. He'll be allowed to keep in touch with you when you go and live with your new family."

"What about Rudy?"

"Well, if we're lucky, some families accept two siblings."

The novelty of the bone china and biscuits became irrelevant. I felt uncomfortable, if not irritated. These qualified adults with a common plan had me cornered. I was a cuffed prisoner without a voice.

They each took turns attempting to convince me of the greater good. I listened but remained unconvinced.

JP wouldn't want us to separate. They are lying. I can't agree and let this happen. I have a Mum. I have a family. Speak up.

"Can I stay here a bit longer until JP leaves, and then look for a family with Rudy, maybe at a later time?"

Claude addressed my question.

"Okay, let's see how it goes. We'll talk about this again in six weeks or so. In the meantime, we'll start looking for candidates. We know some really great foster parents who would love you like their own. You will be so much happier in a foster family, Vital. Think about it."

"What about my mum?"

"Well, as you know, your mum isn't well and was judged by a court incapable of taking care of you."

Those words, though true, pierced my heart and created a lump in my throat that wanted to burst.

I relived the ambulance scene, blood running down Mum's thigh, and Mum and Dad fighting in the hallway as if all were happening right now. The most damning memory was the echo of my words when I condemned Mum to the judge.

Your Honor, I would like to say that everything my brothers told the court is the truth, the whole truth and nothing but the truth, so help me God. God didn't help me that day, though. I shall have to fend for myself today.

I cleared my throat.

"I still have a mum that loves me, even if she's not perfect. I love my Mum and won't love a substitute. I don't need another mum or fake new family to play pretend. You can't separate us, and I won't go."

"Vital," Auntie Ena sighed in astonishment. "That's unlike you to be rude."

"We have the right to do what's best for you, Vital. You are still a child," Claude reminded me.

I warned them that if they separated us, I'd run away and never come back.

"Where will you run to?"

"If I tell you, you'll know where to find me, so why would I tell you?" I exclaimed.

"Mind your tongue, young man," Auntie Ena warned me.

"There is no need to raise your voice. We'll talk about this again in six weeks and introduce you to some lovely candidates. I'm sure you'll like them."

"I won't leave my brothers, and I won't accept a step-mum. Good luck finding me when I've run away!"

I stood up, exited the room, slamming the door behind me.

"I hate this place!" I shouted down the hallway.

I sulked in my bedroom wishing Mum were here, expecting Auntie Ena to come and convince or console me. Nobody came to assure me all would be okay.

I hate this place.

I stared out the window and watched the committee leave in the rain and brooded for the remainder of the afternoon. Mark came to cheer me up.

"Leave me alone!"

Who do they think they are, and what rights do they have over my life? They are neither my mother, my father, nor my big brothers. They are the enemy. They are puppet masters pretending to care. They should mind their own business and stay out of mine.

These psychology graduates were only book savvy numbskulls and couldn't know what it felt like to wear the shoes of rejection and internal frowns of fear. It was hell. It was worse than being a scared, blind, unattended puppy without a teat to suck on. I didn't want to live in the countryside with a pretend Mum and Dad who were paid to parent. Real parents don't get paid, but pay a price. Parents sacrifice, love, protect, and nurture free of charge.

They had taught me a new emotion. Resentment. I resented them and would rebel.

Six weeks later, the issue was readdressed. Once again, I stood up for my convictions.

My stubbornness claimed its reward. They dropped the subject. Even better, Claude left and probably logged his closing report into my file for the next social worker to evaluate.

Mum was right, stand up for your beliefs. The purpose of life seems to be to learn lesson after lesson…and to hurt inside.

CHAPTER 13

Two years had now passed since I moved to Howard's Lane. I'd soon be ten, and plenty had changed. Life became more confusing.

Was I black? Was I British, Belgian, or African? Why the home? Why me?

In all that time since moving here, I'd only seen Mum once or twice. She went back to live in Brussels. Uncle Derrick left, too. Everybody seemed to leave. I missed his Elvis impressions and the camping trips he took us boys on. My best friend, Mark, and his sister, Alison, also left. Their empty beds were quickly filled with unknown faces with similar stories.

Simon Baitner, a twelve-year-old Pakistani boy, and Andrew O'Brian, a fifteen-year-old Irish boy who still wet the bed, were my new roommates.

My new neighbors in the room next door were three young boys, Ricky Dees, David Matcliff, and Mark Long.

Ricky Dees was seven, light-skinned, skinny, and very athletic. David Matcliff was seven, as well, and a dark chocolate brown. He sucked his middle fingers when he slept, leaving his front teeth undeveloped. We poked fun at him, of course. Mark Long had a blacker than black complexion with short nappy hair and always had a runny nose.

"That's snot nice," we taunted.

His younger sister, Michel, wore thick glasses.

"'Ow many bleeedin' milk bottles did ya need to make those glasses, Michel?"

Though we teased and taunted, we loved each other. We were all we had until it was time to move on. Even my favorite teacher, Miss Eaton, moved on to another school. She kept in touch, though, encouraging me to read.

Last year she gave me *The Wind in the Willows* by Kenneth Graham for my birthday. It's about a toad and his animal friends. The story stimulated my imagination. Miss Eaton even took me to the theatre to see a play called *Toad of Toad Hall*, based on the same Kenneth Graham character. I found the theatre magical. I wondered how one joined. I wanted to do it. She also took me to the opera and ballet. What a life those performers must have.

My P.E teacher, Mr. McClean, a good friend of Miss Eaton, took an interest in me, too. He invited me to watch him play cricket during the summer holidays. His wife, Mandy, prepared delicious cucumber sandwiches. The home even allowed me to spend weekends with them and their black Labrador, Vickie. That Christmas, they were taking me up to Lancashire and Cumbria in the north of England to meet their parents. It would be like a family Christmas. I had forgotten what those felt like.

Mum wrote, in broken English, every now and again from Belgium. I came to not miss her.

Ricky and I became best friends. We always played soccer and cricket together. As friendly sports rivals, we made each other better. I planned to play soccer professionally one day, and score the winning goal for England in the world cup final against Brazil.

Andrew continued to wet the bed, and I experienced my second sexual encounter with his sister Mary. The first happened at St. Vincent's, age five or six, when I told a girl sitting next to me at the back of the class that I'd show her mine if she showed me hers. What a surprise to see she didn't have one.

As for my encounter with Mary, she showed me her breasts when we secretly met on the second floor passageway that connected the two houses. I'd never seen naked breasts before, except in a dirty magazine. She let me touch them. They were small and very firm. Her nipples were rosy pink and stood out like antennas. She even showed me what was up her nighty. She had a lot of hair, which made me giggle. I showed her my willy, and it got bigger and felt good. Girls weren't so bad, after all. We often played doctor and nurse until she and her brother left Howard's Lane.

A new girl by the name of Debbie Greenwood replaced Mary. She, like Ricky and me, was "half-caste." We related to each other and bonded instantly. Debbie could be the sister I didn't have, the mother I had lost, and the girl I hoped to marry one day.

She was thirteen, short, with a well-developed backside, large breasts, and a stunning face.

"She's a nice piece of crumpet," the older boys would say, including my brothers.

"I'd like to shag her," said a staff member once.

Shagging girls sounds disgusting!

Debbie's Afro dwarfed mine. To tease me, she'd rub her enormous puffy hair in my face. Despite her beauty, she always wore lots of make-up and high heel shoes, which the new warden, Sally, disapproved of.

Even though smoking was forbidden, she did it all the time to spite the staff, in particular Sally, who she hated.

"If you insist on smoking, we'll have no choice but to send you to Juvenile," warned Sally.

"You bloody smoke more than I do," Debbie replied.

"I am an adult! Besides, mind your language and take off that cheap red lipstick. And spit out that gum and learn to act like a lady, not a slag."

"Why you always picking on me?"

"Act like a responsible adult and I won't pick on you. Now, grow up!"

"Grow up? I'm only thirteen for fuck's sake."

"I beg your pardon, young lady. Go to your room and stay there till you grow some manners."

I found adults to be so hypocritical, even though I hated cigarette smoke and agreed with Sally that Debbie should stop. I did find it cool when Debbie made smoke rings with her mouth, except when she aimed them at me.

"They're love circles, V," she said.

"Get lost. I hate it when you blow them up my nose."

The more Sally disciplined Debbie the more she rebelled, oftentimes running away.

We spent lots of time together, talking about everything and nothing, revealing our secrets, fears and sadness.

"So, where do you go when you run away?" I asked.

"It depends. Sometimes, I go down to King's Cross Station till I meet somebody who will put me up for the night. Or I go to a friend's house."

"What about money?"

"If I tell you, promise you won't tell?"

"Cross my fingers, hope to die."

"I'm a prostitute."

I didn't know what prostitute meant. She explained.

"Oh, you're a slag," I replied.

"Yes, a *slag,*" she said with a hint of shame.

"But you're only thirteen."

"Like I said, you can't tell anybody."

She went on to confess how she sometimes accepted drugs or alcohol for payment.

"The drugs make it all go away. You should try it."

Her stories made me wonder if Mum slept with men for money or food. I thought of the greasy cook from the restaurant below who often gave us food. The idea made me want to run away with Debbie and do drugs. I fancied her, so why not elope? Maybe I'd get the courage to ask her for a kiss while we roamed the streets.

Her lips were lovely and inviting, even without the bargain red lipstick. She actually tried to kiss me once while puffing on a cigarette. I so wanted to, but turned my face away and coughed. If I ever get really lucky, maybe we'll meet on the second floor passageway and she'll show me hers like Mary did. I might show her mine, too.

A few days later Debbie ran away again. I assumed she'd be back within days, as usual. Days turned into weeks without news. Rumor had it she committed suicide by overdose.

I planned to run away. If only there had been a circus in town.

CHAPTER 14

Despite my anger and sadness due to Debbie's suicide, I aced my grades at Sacred Heart with the support and guidance of my favorite teachers, Miss Eaton and Mr. McClean. Those grades allowed me to choose one of many grammar schools in London listed in a graduation booklet Sacred Heart provided.

"Well done, Vital," Sally said. "You should be proud."

The accomplishment felt empty without Mum. I had done it for her and still wanted her to be proud of me, though often convincing myself my love and need for her had died. As for the staff, it didn't matter what they thought or felt. None of them genuinely cared anyway. They related even less. How could they? They were all white. Fortunately, all that lack of relating changed when the home finally hired a black person.

Comfort stood tall and proud, with a long elegant neck, dark, shiny skin with a hint of blue, teeth like pearls, and a pronounced accent from somewhere in Africa. She wore beads, bracelets, and lots of silver. Her affectionate soul displayed strength with softness. She had the same high cheekbones and small flat nose as Mum. Her face bore designed cultural scars. I loved and trusted Comfort and could talk with her about my ethnic confusion.

"You are black and beautiful, Vital!" she said.

"Yeah, but what about my country?"

"Africa is a lovely continent. You must visit it one day and see for yourself."

In terms of physical splendor such as plains and wildlife, I agreed with her, but I had seen on the news and documentaries that corruption and poverty dogged Africa.

"Yes, unfortunately, our homeland is plagued with depravity and poverty," she said.

"Then how on earth can I be proud?"

She continued to clarify, speaking with passion and conviction like a wise storyteller.

"Well, our beautiful continent is also full of riches and natural wonders. They have diamonds, minerals, and incredible palaces. There are big cities and wonderful monuments. And the tribe's people are striking."

"Yeah, but they live in huts and rain dance half naked with spears."

"Oh, Vital! Shame on you!"

"Well, that's what they teach us at school, and I've seen it on telly, as well."

She winced in disbelief.

"That's in bad books written by the white man. Africa is beautiful. It has rituals and traditions that honor and respect the laws of nature. What's wrong with that?"

"Nothing."

"Then never be ashamed of being black or African. Always stand tall and let your color shine."

I hoped she'd stay at Howard's Lane forever, or at least until after the summer holidays.

"Are you gonna leave Howard's Lane, too?" I asked.

"Not yet. I have much more love to share before that time but, eventually, yes."

"Will you take me with you, or at least to my new school on the first day of term?"

"If I'm on duty, of course. It would be my pleasure, my honor."

Britain experienced a record-breaking heat wave that summer of 1976. The daunting dilemma of school outweighed the heat and turbulent political climate. Punk Rock and skinheads were all the rage, yet Abba's "Dancing Queen" topped the British charts. IRA bombs exploded regularly in the heart of London, and the official racist political party, The National Front, gained popularity. Their bigoted rhetoric scared the living daylights out of me. They urged all ethnics to "go *black* home where we belong." I didn't have a home to go "black" to.

By mid-August, I couldn't handle the anticipation of who would take me to school.

"Sally, can Comfort please be on duty to take me to school?"

"I haven't done the schedule yet. You'll have to wait and see."

"Please. I don't want my new school to know I live in an 'ome. If Comfort takes me, they'll fink she's my mum and ask no questions? Can you please schedule her?"

"I said you'll have to wait and see," Sally reiterated, ending the conversation.

Either way, I had already decided to do whatever it took to appear like a normal boy with a mum and dad at my new school. Nobody there would ever find out about my residential disgrace.

September arrived too soon, which was great in one sense, because I'd celebrate my twelfth birthday, but horrifying with regard to that dreaded first school day.

Instead of the "black is beautiful" Comfort taking me, John, a white, long-haired, self-proclaimed hippie accompanied me. Though John was a cool cat who played electric guitar and could whistle real loud through the gap in his front teeth, he'd give me away. And for that, I disliked him.

Why didn't Sally simply put Comfort on duty? Debbie was right; Sally was a hypocritical, selfish bitch without a heart. What did she care who took me to school or if the kids at school found out.

As the other parents walked their sons into the assembly hall, I pretended to not know John and kept a distance. An Irish boy named Shaun sat next to me.

"Is that yer ol' man?" he whispered while the soft-spoken Headmaster addressed his new congregation.

"Parents, pupils," he said, as if walking on water with his palms open like the Messiah himself. "Welcome to Salesian (suh/lee-zian) College Catholic Secondary School for Boys."

His assistant stood next to him like a voracious centurion in search of a victim. The remaining faculty sat behind them.

I told Shaun the *'ol' man* was my uncle.

"Me mum and dad couldn't make it. He's my Uncle John."

A technical truth, as the home made us address the staff as uncles and aunts.

"'E needs an 'aircut," Shaun joked.

I changed the subject immediately, after sniggering.

"Silence!" yelled the Assistant Headmaster.

His deep loud voice reverberated around the hall, eyes bulging, forehead wrinkled. His bald scalp filled with blood as he dared us to utter another sound. We all understood not to mess with *him*. We soon learned from senior pupils his nickname was appropriately "Baldy". His official title was Dean of Discipline.

Instead of waving good-bye to parents at the end of assembly, or hugging like all the other pupils did, I ignored John and hid. I didn't want to be seen or associated with him.

CHAPTER 15

Shadowing the Headmaster's welcome speech, The Dean of Discipline explained we were to exit the assembly hall in absolute silence and head to the playground.

Our form teacher, Father Docherty, met us outside. He lined us up in order of height. I stood the shortest, but taller than him, and abided at the front. I turned to Shaun behind me and whispered.

"Man United are gonna lick Chelsea this season, man."

"Bollocks?" Shaun whispered back, flicking his two V-shaped fingers at me.

"What's your name, young man?" Father Docherty yelled.

"Jacob, Sir."

"You will address me as Father Docherty or simply Father, and not sir. Is that clear? I said, is that clear everybody?"

"Yes, Father Docherty," the class responded in unison.

"And what's your friend's name with the vulgar tongue and fingers?"

"Shaun, Sir, eh, I mean, Father." he answered.

"Good! Now, Mr. Jacob, if I hear you speak once more without my permission, you will be my first victim and a prime example as to what happens to little boys who cannot control their tongues."

I felt a rush of blood to my face and knew it had turned a dark crimson. I hoped not all the priests were this strict.

Father Docherty looked like an old toad with his furrowed features and large eyes. He was the Salesian Toad of Toad Hall and just as miserable. He continued.

"And mark my words, class One Alpha, you do not wish to find out what Father Docherty does to petulant little boys who speak out of turn when they should be seen and not heard. Clear?"

"Yes, Father Docherty," the class responded.

We marched in complete hush down the long covered courtyard. Though still September and reasonably sunny for England, it smelled of damp and cat urine. Lush gardens separated us from what looked like a chapel to our left. The main building, a bit further down, towered over the oratory like a disgruntled grandparent. Gothic arches and narrow windows gave it the look of an old church, or castle even. The outer walls were aged; red brick turned black and partially covered with vines and ivy. We could have been at Oxford University. I felt proud, if not snobby, to be a *Salesian*.

Just before we arrived at the main doors, Father Docherty turned and raised his palm to us. We stopped. He reminded us of the importance of silence before opening the gates to the dragon's lair. We followed him up the stairs to our classroom. An engraved bronze plaque atop the timeworn, pale blue door read, "Class 1 Alpha."

I sat next to Shaun in the first row and observed all the other pupils. We all wore the same maroon blazer, red sweater, and maroon tie with yellow and red diagonal stripes. Most had on a white shirt, though a few wore the optional grey. Several wore spectacles, looking like young scientists. Everybody had the same black briefcase. I had the only black face.

We began with prayer. Initiation and teacher introductions completed the day. At 3:30 p.m. the bell rang, much to my relief.

"See ya tomorra', Shaun."

"Later, mate."

I had survived the first day of school, and nobody was the wiser regarding Howard's Lane.

Thank you, God.

I couldn't wait for tomorrow. I had so much to talk about with Shaun, plus we had soccer trials.

CHAPTER 16

Salesian College was located in Battersea, South London, on the banks of the Thames and named after St. Francis of Sales. The priests who ran it were of the *Don Bosco* order and were all apparently very strict and enjoyed silence.

School started at 9:15 a.m. precisely, and I had two transportation options to get there. The first, the number 37 red, classic, double-decker bus. It ambled through polluted streets and congested sights to my destination, Clapham Junction. I sat by the second story window looking down at the worker-ants on their humdrum routes. Their banal conformity entertained my vivid imagination. I fantasized that they, too, were lost and confused with challenges. Surely, we kids in the home weren't the only ones suffering from circus freak syndrome.

Most of these anonymous passersby lived a life unnoticed. I wanted my life to have meaning. I would prove to the home that Vital was not another statistic heading for failure but destined for something great that would one day make all my suffering worthwhile.

"Any more fares, please," yelled the conductor.

I flashed my pink pass. He continued collecting money from others.

The second transportation option was quicker, but far less stimulating. The British Rail train meandered overground across viaducts on its way to the city center.

Both train and bus were filled with chain-smoking passengers in a hurry to get to professional commitments. Most politely gazed at sweet nothings avoiding awkward eye contact. Others typically read newspapers, which was more common to the tube of central London, filled with its bowler-hat-wearing English gentlemen. From Clapham Junction, I walked a mile to school.

The first couple of months at Salesian's went by smoothly, managing to keep my secret. Shaun and I became best friends. He often invited me over to his house. I never reciprocated. My home was not a home.

"I really like your mum and dad. They're cool cats. You're pretty lucky, Shaun."

"They're alright, I guess. What er your mum and dad like?"

I knew this moment would come sooner or later, yet there I sat unprepared on the school bus heading to our soccer match.

"Well, I'm not quite as lucky as you are."

"What eh you talkin' about?"

"Shaun, can you keep a secret mate."

"'Course I can. Who do ya fink I am, the Daily Mirror?"

Shaun always had wit but, for me, this was no laughing matter. I panicked for a moment, before somehow sputtering the words out of my mouth, confessing about Howard's Lane.

"Is that like an orphanage or somefin'?"

"Kinda, but not really."

"So where's ya mum and dad?"

Though I told him the truth about Mum living in Belgium for health reasons, I lied about my father.

"So why didn't you just go back wiv 'er?"

"'Cause she wanted me to go to school 'ere in England. She says it's the best education in the world."

"Right. God save the Queen, an all that rubbish. What's in Belgium?"

"I don't know, really. Chocolate and waffles, I fink."

"Waffles, what the fuck's that?"

"It's a Belgian kind of biscuit that could be a cake made from pancake mix. They're pretty tasty, I'll tell ya that much. Next time my mum visits, I'll bring ya some."

"Nicely done, mate; good on ya."

For the remainder of the bus ride we talked about soccer. I hoped he'd forget my confession ever happened. He didn't. After the match and before arriving back at Salesian's, he reminded me that my secret sat safe with him.

For the remainder of the year, the routine of everyday life took shape at Salesian College. Shaun christened me Jake, short for Jacob, my original last name. The nickname stuck with me throughout the school years. Even some of the teachers referred to me as Jake. I found that pretty nifty.

I always looked forward to P.E., disliked religion, and found art and English boring. Saturday morning soccer matches were the highlight of the week, even during the bitter, rainy, winter mornings when my toes lost all sensation and my fingers turned blue from frost.

Bloody British weather.

For the next semesters, I did everything to blend in. The more I tried, the more I struggled. The more I struggled, the more confused and pubescent I acted. I challenged everybody and everything, including religion and authority. My grades deteriorated.

"So why does God allow war and innocent people to die horrible deaths, Father?"

The sentiment related to Debbie, who must have died lonely and afraid under the influence.

"Because He gave us free will as His chosen race," the priest responded.

He made a sign of the cross and looked up.

"Jacob, you should know better than to question His word. Please stay after school to write out a hundred times, I shall not question the word of God. Shame on you."

"Why you always pickin' on me?"

"Make that two hundred times, unless you wish to add any further petulance."

When I'd exhausted his lines and he realized they didn't affect me, he hit me with his feared-by-all lethal weapon, "The Daniel Jazz". It's a poem by Vachel Lindsay that went on and on and on, page after page of prophetic verses about lions and worship. Writing out that poem ten times constituted religious persecution unto itself.

After class, Shaun asked me what the home said about all my detentions.

"They don't care," I replied.

It had only been months since I shared my secret with him, but I wished I hadn't. I feared he would betray me since making a few open snide remarks about my parents. Pupils gossiped. From one day to the next, he and all my friends turned on me, making me the orphan circus freak that should be avoided. Lunchtime and recess became exercises in overcoming alienation. Never again would I trust anybody.

Overnight I grew to detest Salesian College, the home and the staff. I hated life! I wanted to run away, but acted out instead.

The more I behaved like a typical dysfunctional boy in childcare, the more concern the staff expressed regarding my indifference and rude contempt for authority. I became the very statistic I had fought. Destined to fail, yet determined to succeed and fulfill my dreams.

CHAPTER 17

"What happened to the well-mannered Vital we all liked so well?" asked Sally.

Knowing my answer was inappropriate, I kept it to myself and remained civilly disobedient. My gentle nature always got the better of me.

Sally set up a meeting with my new social worker. More questions and more psychological evaluations were pelted at me. Feeling like nothing more than an assignment, my cynicism spiked. I played mind games.

"How is school coming along?" asked my social worker.

"The custard ain't what it used to be cause the price of eggs went up."

He appeared puzzled at my out of context response. He glanced at his notes, placed his hand to his mouth and cleared his throat. How he looked escapes me. His presence and appearance were meaningless. Social workers had become a formality I tolerated and ignored like homework.

"We would like to talk about your current behavior - and your childhood, in particular your mother and father."

They didn't seem to grasp the impossibility to helping something they didn't understand and I knew they could never comprehend.

"Are you aware of what happened to your father?"

"Yeah, e got arrested and got sent back to Belgium."

"Do you know why?"

I played tough, though I didn't really know for sure. Mum, JP and Rudy never openly talked about it, but I kind of knew. I answered with an assertive, "Yes."

"Did your mother ever touch you in a sexual way?"

Why are they asking such a question about my mum? What bastards!

"What kind of question is that?" I raised my voice. "But, no, she did not, if you must know!"

"We're only trying to help, Vital."

"Help? Ya fink you know me, but you don't, so stay out of my business and leave me alone."

They would never have the opportunity to know who I really was, what I cried for, or what I laughed at. Nobody would know about my nightmares.

Besides, the caseworkers always used my personal information against me. It validated their theory that I needed the safe haven of foster parents. I still had a mother and father.

"Did your mother ever sleep with you in the same bed or touch you in a way that made you feel uncomfortable?"

I headed for the door in disgust.

"Good luck with your bleedin' report," I stated before slamming the door behind me, attempting to crack it in half.

Sally chased me down the hallway.

"How dare you walk out like that, Vital. Now get back inside, right away."

"Piss off!"

"I beg your pardon."

She asked me to calm down and explain what I felt, assuring me she was on my side.

"If you actually listened and cared, I might, but you all never listen. You don't 'ear us, ya know what I mean? You don't even give a toss, so what's the point?"

Everybody at the home hated social workers and the

interviews. What a waste of time. But we *were* all very curious as to what they wrote in our files. Under normal circumstances, we'd be allowed to read a censored version at the age of eighteen, when we were no longer under the control of social services. I read mine prematurely.

A very open-minded or defiant staff member, depending on how one looks at it, allowed me to read it. The uncensored version and its revelations were shocking.

The harsh and surprising information concerning my mother's alcoholism was hard to sip and swallow. I knew she drank, but I'd never heard the term alcoholic in reference to her. Shame consumed me.

My mum's an alcoholic.

The circumstances behind my father's arrest were harder still to read. He had officially been accused of sexually manipulating JP, Rudy, and me and sent to jail before extradition to Belgium. Nobody knew or cared what he had become or where he ran to escape his demons.

My grades went to the bottom of the pile, my self-esteem even lower.

Like a sad clown, a fake painted smile masked my despair. The tears of solitude that resided in my personal backstage I dabbed with denial, leaving only room for dreams.

CHAPTER 18

By the time I reached the fourth form at age fifteen, JP had been gone from Howard's Lane for a couple of years. He married and worked for a firm called British Telecom and lived in a small two-bedroom flat in Streatham, South London. Rudy moved in with him while he navigated independence from social services. He worked several jobs such as Amway and McDonalds, during the onset of their British invasion. Rudy loved everything American and planned to move there.

The only person who didn't move away was the warden, Sally, who now regularly invited her lesbian lover, Gwen, to drink whisky in front of the telly and have sleepovers.

As the oldest boy, I had my own room up in the attic and enjoyed the privilege and privacy of the top floor. It had it's own bathroom and slanted ceilings. I covered the walls with posters of Bruce Lee, Michael Jackson, and Manchester United. It became my sanctuary.

My grades improved considerably that mid-term, proving I could be as good as anybody else. Mr. McLean invested plenty of time, pushing me to do homework and revise before exams.

Oku Benligufwa became my new best friend. He stood an athletic six-feet. He had been in class since the onset but, despite his light complexion, I never noticed him due to his withdrawn behavior.

"You're black?"

"Well, half-caste. My mum's Irish and my dad's Nigerian."

"You're the first black Irishman I've ever met, mate. Top eh the mornin' to ya with Afro combs, voodoo, and hot sauce."

By default, I seemed to gravitate toward people with similar racial backgrounds. Us half-castes had to stick together lest go "black" home to somewhere we didn't even belong. We became inseparable.

Life passed smoothly for a while. Oku often visited Howard's Lane and didn't pass judgment. We played Subbuteo in my room for hours and listened to soul music. We hung out at his house a lot, too. His mum frequently cooked sausage, eggs and chips with baked beans, and toast covered in rich creamy butter, followed by a good cup of tea and chocolate biscuits.

His tall very dark-skinned father was rarely home. I developed a secret crush on both his elder sisters. He also had a baby brother.

At school, I took an interest in law and journalism, aspiring to go to university. I was content. It had been a good year, but fleeting changes took place, accelerating life into a new era. Margaret Thatcher became the first woman Prime Minister of England, Rhodesia changed its name to Zimbabwe, Rudy turned very pro-African, if not a racist black activist, and JP became a dad. More importantly, a group of Oxford University students performed the first modern bungee jump. There was no trapeze used that day.

Rudy often invited me to attend his black activist meetings at The Pan African Congress Movement. We collectively researched Negro history and discovered endless notable, scientific, and medical achievements of the "black man."

One book revealed that the first successful open heart surgery was done by a Negro, Dr. Daniel Hale William.

Wow! There is more to us than rain dances, ignorant smelly slaves, and criminals.

Further literature on Marcus Garvey, Martin Luther King and the racially charged Malcom X provided uplifting knowledge. Alex Hailey's *Roots* TV series, on the other hand, did not lift my spirits. It ignited a fury inside me. My already developing angst toward the blue-eyed devil peaked.

I wanted to kill every white man or woman I came across and struck pork from my menu. Considering ninety-nine percent of the people surrounding me were Caucasian, including Oku's lovely mum and Mr. McClean, it put me in shackles of conflict and confusion.

By the end of fourth-form, Rudy departed for America.

"Don't leave me behind. Take me with you," I pleaded.

"I'll be back in no time. Stay tuff, stay black."

"Okay, but hurry "black" home."

"Asalam Malaykum, lil' bruva'."

"Malaykum-Asalam, big brother."

JP appeared too busy for me, taking care of his wife and baby, my niece, Natasha. I desperately needed his support, but remained too immature to understand he had to live his life and become a functioning adult and start his own family.

There was nobody to turn to. The teachers couldn't care; they taught, not parented. As for the home, nothing changed. I focused on my eighteenth birthday when the cuffs of childcare would legally lose their grasp. Just two more years and I'd be free like Chicken George.

The un-sweet age of sixteen would pass, surely!

Another typical Salesian day ended, except I didn't have detention. Oku and I walked down to Clapham Junction together in the rain, talking about Subbuteo and whether or not The Jackson's were better than Earth, Wind and Fire, his favorite group.

"Shit man, there's my bus. See ya tomorra' Tito," he said, running after his bus.

"I'm Michael, you bastard. Tito's bloody rubbish, just like Earth, Wind and Fire."

I waited over an hour for the bus to Putney, arriving home late and missing out on supper. Ricky and I played table tennis. I ignored my homework.

That next January morning at about 8:00 a.m., I made desperate touches to my ignored homework when a voice from below yelled out.

"Yu wot?" I responded.

"You've got a long distance call from Belgium. You can take it in the staff room."

"Right, right, cheers. I'll be down in a sec."

At first, I presumed it was Mum on the line announcing a visit and rushed downstairs in heightened expectation. I picked up the beige phone receiver and spoke to an unknown Belgian woman. She could not express in English, and I couldn't understand enough French.

The gist of the conversation suggested for me to go to Belgium urgently—something to do with Mum.

I hung up the phone and called JP at his job.

"I think the lady said Mum was really ill and that I needed to visit immediately."

"Mum's gonna be fine. I'll call the home's administration tomorrow, and we'll make plans to go next week or something."

"Mum's seriously ill, John. Don't give me that Cool Hand Luke crap."

He probably meant to soothe my anxiety with his calm words of logic, but the part about going next week to visit seemed more like a sign of indifference.

"Next week. Why next week and not now, for Pete's sake?" I asked.

"You can't miss school just like that, Jake."

"My friends call me Jake, not you! Rudy would have cared if he were here!"

I hung up and hid in my attic room with no intention of going to school. I felt JP held resentment toward Mum for all she had miscarried. She had indeed failed us, but we shouldn't fail *her*. I went back downstairs and got permission to call JP back.

"It's me, again."

The childcare authorities wouldn't let me travel to Belgium without a Spanish Inquisition. With his presence as my legal guardian, there hung a slim chance they'd allow me to travel. During his years at the home, JP had demonstrated impeccable responsibility. They loved and respected him. He agreed to chaperone me.

"Cheers, JP. I love you, man."

The necessary powers at the Childcare Services head office were not available when I called. I spoke with a secretary.

"I can take a message if you like," she said.

"How long will it take for them to respond to that message?"

"Usually a couple of weeks; besides, you and your warden will have to fill out a petition."

Bureaucratic protocol sucked. I explained the situation in more detail, hoping she'd sympathize and fast track my request.

"I am sorry, but there is nothing I can do. What message would you like to leave?"

"That, um, am I supposed to sit, wait, and cross my fingers while my mum dies? I haven't seen her in over a year and might never see her again."

There was a long pause. "Just give me a moment."

Later that evening, I met JP at Victoria Station. We took the boat-train to Dover and boarded a ferry to Belgium. And so began a life-changing five-day trip that had nothing to do with chocolate.

CHAPTER 19

The four-hour ferry gave me ample time to reflect and feel nausea. The prospect of life as an orphan burdened my mind, inviting self-pity.

We arrived in Ostend, Belgium at 5:00 a.m., followed by the formalities of customs. Agents pulled us aside, searched our luggage, and questioned us. I speculated if our color had anything to do with it. We were, after all, the only black people onboard and the only ones questioned. It could also have been because I appeared more like a twelve-year-old stowaway and not a young man in the second half of his teens. I had once overheard a social worker refer to me as physically immature, and I hated that reality. Looking four years younger than my actual age humiliated me.

JP and I walked down the cold corridors to a small opening. A white woman signaled from a distance to join her. Somehow, she knew who we were. Again, I assumed color gave us away, or my huge Afro that almost stood taller than me.

"Allo, me Marcella," she greeted us with a very thick French accent.

"You, Vital?"

"Yes, *oui. Bonjour.*"

She looked at JP.

"Jean-Pierre?"

Marcella gave us three kisses on alternating cheeks,

before speaking with my brother in French. I listened, understanding the odd word here and there.

Her long, curly hair revealed hints of grey, partially covering her very pale parched face. She had a tiny nose, tight narrow lips, and sunken eyes with dark rings beneath them.

She escorted us to a bright, lime-green Volkswagen van outside. The engine ran. The exhaust left a visible trail in the bitter winter air. The sea haze added to the obscure, frosty walk across the cobblestoned parking lot.

An old bearded gentleman sat at the driver's side on the left, which to me was the wrong side. He wore a navy officer's cap, thick glasses, and a silk scarf neatly tucked under his chin. The details of his profile were undefined and broken in the shadows cast by the street lamps.

We sat in the back with Marcella, who introduced the man as an old friend of our mother's. He didn't turn his head but simply raised his hand and said, "Allo', well komen to Belgee-um," his accent even thicker than Marcella's. "No speken English, me forgiving, please."

A small, light-skinned girl aged about fourteen, wearing a raincoat with fur on the hood, sat next to the mysterious figure. Marcella introduced her as the man's daughter, Mireille.

We drove along dark, winding roads of the Belgian coast for about thirty minutes, passing by gloomy dunes and through several quaint sleepy towns before arriving at our destination. During the commute, the chauffeur remained quiet, excluding a few odd comments made to his daughter who mumbled back. JP and Marcella continued to chat. I just wanted to see Mum. The thought of her dying horrified me. Though she'd been far away, life without her seemed unimaginable. I couldn't wait to hold her.

We entered another small town and drove along tramlines.

"Welcome to 'Blankenbergghhe'," said Marcella.

The name sounded like a glottal disorder that would need surgery.

The dark, empty town sat silent in the early morning drizzle. Windows showed no sign of light or life.

"Ah, we're here. This is our home," she added moments later as we pulled up to a house on a narrow street.

Marcella invited us into a warm living room. The mantelpiece above the fireplace stood decorated with bombshells and bullets. Two crossed swords hung above the military memorabilia. A robust shield claimed center stage. The sofa and chairs were new with vintage floral upholstery. I presumed Mum slept upstairs, and I'd see her at last. We sat down. The bearded fellow remained standing, addressing us in French.

"I am an old friend of your mother's and have known her for over twenty years." He paused. "She wants me to tell you that she loves you very much, Vital."

Those words felt so good. He continued.

"Your father was not the evil man she portrayed him to be, and your father loves you very much, too—more than you can imagine. He has always loved you."

JP translated. The man went on.

"Your mother regrets depriving your father of his son for all these years. She wishes to repair the damage."

His next sentence paralyzed me.

"Your mother died two weeks ago. I am sorry."

Then came the Hollywood shocker moment.

"And I am your father!"

CHAPTER 20

The man, my father, had tears in his eyes, as did Marcella and Mireille. He opened his arms, inviting me to embrace him.

What? You're my father? My mum died two weeks ago and you only called me yesterday?

He looked at the young girl and winked.

"*Tonton*. May I call you *Tonton*?"

"*Oui*."

"Mireille is your mother's daughter. She is my daughter, too, and your full-blood sister."

What? I have a sister? A sister nobody has ever heard about? When was Mum pregnant? Why wouldn't she have told us?

She looked just like Debbie, the sister I never had. Mireille was shorter than me, with an Afro, and a tiny nose. Her skin was a couple of shades paler than mine, and her big, dark brown eyes were piercing.

"Jean-Pierre, you're my son, too. When I adopted you I did it like you were my own flesh," the man added.

JP's stunned eyes were as much in the headlights as mine. He stood up and embraced the man. I had just lost a mum and gained a dad? It didn't seem like a fair trade. I wanted to shed a tear, but didn't. My stomach tightened; my mouth dried.

"Tonton, my son, you haven't changed. You have the same gentle face and soft eyes as I remember from the last time I saw you when you were only three-years-old."

Are you really my father? The same man who I read once upon a time sexually violated our innocence and was arrested and extradited from England. Why didn't my brother recognize you?

"You look like your mum," Marcella advised me.

"Thank you."

Mireille held my hand and put her head on my shoulder.

Marcella disappeared into the kitchen to prepare coffee, while my newly declared father told stories about his past. He seemed like a wonderful man. I had apparently missed out on a beautiful childhood. My heart ached for Mum, yet I felt a flood of resentment toward her for the love, life, and dad she had deprived me of.

Shortly after this stunning revelation, Marcella came back in with the coffee and a group of sleepy children.

"These are my children, your father's children," Marcella said as she placed the tray on the table.

The man catered the introductions.

"This is Jeannine, the eldest, and this is Carol."

"Carol is good at gymnastics. I am proud of my daughter," bragged Marcella as she poured.

The children walked toward me, each giving three kisses on the cheek. JP received them, too. The man continued.

"This is your younger brother, Christophe, who's been dying to meet his big brother. And this little one here, that's Christiane, she's four and the baby."

More kisses were shared. I'd been kissed more in an hour than in my entire life.

My new siblings were gorgeous, with dark-blonde hair, blue eyes and aged approximately four, five, seven, and eight.

"Have you met Diavolino," asked one of the kids.

"*Non,*" I said, frowning with confusion, wondering who or what this Diavolino thing might be.

"*Papa*, can we show Tonton and Jean-Pierre Diavolino?"

He didn't think it a good idea and denied their request.

"*Papa*, please, Tonton wants to see the dog. Please, *Papachoo*."

The man yielded to their innocent demands, showing me a sensitive, caring nature.

They surged out the door with such joy and celebration. Seconds later Diavolino barged in wagging his silky red tail. His tall, thin frame jumped up and licked me all over. He rolled on his back, begging for a tummy rub.

The kids joined in the tummy rub, giggling, shoving and pushing to be a part of the attraction. The Irish Setter sprang to his feet and ran around crazy with all the commotion.

"Okay, enough children. That's enough! Take him back to the cellar," ordered Marcella. "Carol! Take him back, please, now."

It saddened me that such a beautiful, vibrant dog lived in the cellar.

A very short, fragile, old lady with curly, platinum, semi-translucent hair entered. The dog's excited tail whipped her legs, almost knocking her over as Carol escorted him back to his prison. A thick-knitted wool cardigan enveloped the woman's petite frame. The brown sheepskin slippers she dragged with each small step protected her feet from the cold carpet.

"Carol!" yelled Marcella. "Be careful!"

"Shh, it's okay," said the man with a soothing voice. "They are children, he's a dog. They are all very excited to see their brothers, Tonton and Jean-Pierre."

Marcella shrugged, mumbled, and sipped her coffee.

"Are you okay," my father asked the lady who nodded, holding on to the door for stability.

"This is my mother, Bobonne. Your Grandma."

He raised his voice and addressed her.

"Bobonne! This is Tonton and Jean-Pierre!"

"*Je sais*, I know," she muttered.

She walked toward me, fighting to keep her balance. I stepped forward to meet her.

"Ah, my little Tonton, I knew you when you were a baby. You used to always sit on my lap, and I'd rock you to sleep. You haven't changed a bit."

Her frail hands caressed my cheek.

"You have the same soft eyes."

Tears ran down her matured face. She pulled out a handkerchief from her sleeve, wiped her eyes, and blew her nose. She had a very large nose that was even bigger than my dad's.

So that's where I get mine. I hate my nose.

"*Bonjour*, Jean-Pierre," Bobonne said. "Look at you. What a strong young man you've become."

Dad asked Grandma to take the kids into the kitchen and serve breakfast before school, as we had more talking to do.

"*Au revoir*, Tonton. *Au revoir*, Jean-Pierre," yelled the kids, waving their hands and pressing to kiss their dad good-bye.

More kisses followed before they exited. The wave of chaos that had just invaded the living room subsided as if a black hole had swallowed it in a single gulp. We all breathed a sigh of relief.

So this is what love, family, and happiness feels like. I had forgotten.

Though exhausted, I wanted to know more about Mum's final moments.

The man sat down in what was obviously *his* armchair in the corner of the room. He gestured for us to take a seat on the couch, took off his black spectacles, rubbed his eyes, and stroked his groomed peppered beard with care and wisdom. He looked like Sigmund Freud, a psychiatrist I had learned about at school. This was, hopefully, not a neurotic dream.

A deep breath filled Dad's lungs. He placed the glasses back on the bridge of his nose. Mireille sat down on his lap, holding his hand. How Freudian.

"I'm sorry to tell you, but your mother regrettably died a lonely death in a hospital in Brussels from cancer of the liver," he revealed.

I guess the drinking finally took its toll.

He went on. "Her last wish was that I find you, Tonton, and reunite you with your sister, Mireille. And here you are. I have kept my promise and honored your mum's dying wish."

I gazed over at JP. His eyes watered, much to my surprise. The man raised his brows, pinched his lips, and exhaled. Marcella stood silent by the coffee with a cup in her hand, head tilted to the side.

The tick of a large clock filled the space. Mireille stood up, walked over, and sat next to me. We held hands.

"Mireille and Tonton," the man said. "Your mother can smile and rest in peace now that you are together again. Welcome home."

That's when *I* finally cried.

CHAPTER 21

I instantly cherished my long lost family but couldn't decide what to feel. Anger? Joy? Hate or love? I felt everything and nothing dished up with an overdose of confusion.

I can't believe I have a dad! The thought of him had not even crossed my mind on the ferry.

The social service reports affirmed he had been arrested for sexual abuse when I was three, and I do vaguely remember the fights with Mum, yet this man before me, my father, seemed of such a harmless disposition. There must have been a mistake in the file, or was this all too good to be true?

Mum, please come back. No, don't! You deserve what you got.

I probably should have felt anger, but I didn't know how to be angry, it wasn't my nature.

Sorry, Mum, I love you. Wait a minute! My father abused us and, because of him, Mum turned to alcohol and is now dead.

I had every right to hate, but couldn't; that, too, wasn't in my nature.

But, Mum, why did you hide my sister from me all these years? Why didn't you tell Dad where I was? Or is he lying?

There remained only one way to find the truth, as JP wasn't revealing any secrets either. I would have to overcome my shyness and grow the courage to confront my father and ask the right questions. I planned to do it later that evening after I had slept and collected myself.

I can. I will. I must.

CHAPTER 22

"You must be exhausted," Marcella questioned.

"*Non*. I'm fine. *Merci*."

"Okay. *Magnifique!*"

I was indeed spent but too embarrassed to say so. I'd get some sleep when JP decided to.

"Would you like to see the rest of the house?"

JP answered for us both. Marcella began the tour in the adjacent room.

"Okay. Here is the formal dining room."

A luscious chandelier hung over the table. Next to it by the wall stood a glass cabinet filled with pottery and an array of other delicate pieces of bone china and trinkets.

"That's famous Delft pottery from Holland. It's very expensive," bragged Dad. "Holland's a beautiful country but, Dutch, that's one hell of an ugly language. *Les Flemingant* (the dirty Flems), make it even more ugly. They sound like constipated cats clearing hairballs when they attempt to speak."

The visual amused me.

In the corner, a door lent to a tiny outdoor courtyard that catered an extra toilet. Clothes lines crisscrossed overhead. Marcella led us through a sliding partition into the narrow kitchen. Exposed pipes ran every which way. Dad explained his plans to remodel and conceal the plumbing and take out the timeworn bathtub next to the stove. Enthusiasm laced his words. An opening gave way to a casual eating area with refrigerator and a plentiful pantry.

The tour continued into the hallway. The dog barked as we passed his cellar below the stairs.

"*Calme toi,* (calm down) Diavolino," stated my father in a tender melodic tone.

It saddened me that the poor dog sat trapped down there in the dark and cold. All he wanted was love, warmth, and attention.

A unique odor of old age and trapped air lingered in the vestibule. A bunch of bikes boarded the entry way by the front door. Yellowing wallpaper covered the walls.

"Okay, upstairs," sang Marcella. "There are many floors! *On y va* (here we go)."

Just then, four energized kids scampered down eager for school. More kisses, hugs and chaos.

"*Au revoir.* Bye bye," they said hurrying through the door and out into the glacial morning air. Calm followed.

The stairs squeaked as we climbed. An annex located between the first and second floors housed the master bedroom for Marcella and Dad. Grandma lived on the first floor in what was a separate apartment: kitchen, bedroom, living room, water closet, but no tub.

"I'm going to install a second bathroom with a shower here for Grandma and take out this decrepit cooker," Dad said, hugging his mother who put down her knitting and struggled to get out of her rocking chair.

We continued upstairs to the kids' rooms on the third floor. Mireille had her own.

"What's that up there?" I asked.

"Oh, that's the attic. We use it for storage. Nothing to see but junk, really," Dad responded.

Lofts were my favorite, and I wanted to take a look. The three small rooms hidden away with their slanted ceilings and skylights gave me an encouraging sense of familiarity.

"They're just like my room back at the home, right JP?"

He nodded. "Can I come back and visit in the summer? I'll help with the renovations."

"We'll talk about that some other time," replied Dad. "Time for breakfast."

My stomach growled for food, but my appetite dictated otherwise. Endless concerns bobbed and bounced in my brain numbing the need for nutrition.

Marcella served fresh coffee, soft white bread with a selection of cheeses and thin slices of ham. Dad dipped his sandwich, enjoying his soggy morning feast. Grandma sat silent, nibbling like a pigeon with her other half lost in thought. I mirrored her.

As my father masticated away at his sandwich, he shared some touching narratives about the good old days in The Congo.

"*Tonton,* do you remember when I saved you from that Cobra in our back yard?"

I pulled a perplexed grimace, suggesting not. I was too timid and polite to tell him that I was less than six months old when we escaped and couldn't possibly remember.

"Jean-Pierre, surely you remember?"

JP hesitantly said no.

"Ah, that's a shame. Ask anybody. Any of our servants will tell you what your *Papa* did for you, my son. The snake tried to bite me as I pried it from your fragile little body. It was so strong and wouldn't let go; I had to get a machete from the guard and cut its head off. Ask the guard, he'll tell you."

Wow! How brave.

I observed JP's reactions for clues, but his face and eyes revealed nothing.

Half an untouched sandwich remained on my plate. I could eat no more, feeling total embarrassment for my waste. JP must have read my mind and scoffed it for me.

The trumpet blowing continued.

"You *must* remember how I threw myself on top of you, Jean-Pierre, to protect you from an explosion during the Civil War?"

"I guess I must have blocked out those ugly memories; forgive me. I was still very young."

"Do you remember living in that apartment on Welbeck Street in London before your mother and I split?"

"Not really, it's all foggy; my apologies."

At this point, my eyes were closing from fatigue. I lacked the nerve to announce my tiredness, begging JP to once again read my mind. He didn't.

"I need some shut-eye, mate. Don't tell em bruv, please."

He knew exactly what to say.

"Thank you for breakfast, but I think it's time for me and Vital to get some sleep. I'm spent."

Marcella walked us up to our room. JP and I talked for a bit. He conveyed little and answered even less. He went back downstairs, allowing me to rest.

Mum, why did you abandon me and forsake me to the pitiless institutions when I had a dad who would have loved me? How could you?

I got into bed.

I miss you, Mum. Don't leave me; I need you.

Within seconds of placing my head on the pillow, my eyes closed and sleep took over—a rare event. I woke up that evening wondering where on earth I had landed and if the overwhelming revelations had all been a dream. Unfortunately, they weren't. Mum *was* dead. I never even said good-bye.

CHAPTER 23

Suppertime arrived. My questions were well rehearsed. Marcella served a strange vegetable with a disgusting bitter taste I later learned were endives. Delicious roast chicken and French fries with optional mayonnaise rounded off the menu.

"Do you have ketchup?" I asked.

"KETCHUP?" Dad bellowed with a huge grin, sounding just like the warden from Oliver Twist yelling, MORE! "We are Belgians, not Americans. Ketchup is a gastronomic violation. Did you know the big-shot Yanks stole the hamburger from us after the war?

I had no idea.

"Fries aren't even French, they're Belgian."

Who cares? I have important questions to ask.

Confront him! Somebody's lying!

To be polite, I forced down the sordid veggies, thinking that boiled cabbage sounded like a delicacy right about now.

I failed to ask any poignant questions, but planned to ask the next morning at breakfast. That evening, he shared more stories until bedtime. I slept in my sister's room in the sleeper couch. She slept in her bed opposite me, and JP with the younger siblings in the other room.

"Good night, little sister."

"Sleep well, my big brother."

CHAPTER 24

The first days in Belgium with my newfound family were a welcome relief from life in the home, which tendered diminutive love and more silt than the murky depths of the River Thames. So much affection and gentleness existed in this house. It was home and not a home.

What a great dad I have. I'll invite Oku to come and visit when I return this summer. I can't wait to show off my dad.

The words "my dad" sounded glorious. If only Rudy were here. He might grow to like white people again.

That morning, my perfect family took a long stroll on the deserted boardwalk. I held Diavolino, tiring quickly from his endless tug-of-war.

The fine, beige sand stretched far out to where the low tide gently rippled. The grey sea slept calmly with a soft breeze brushing over it. Clouds blanketed the sky. An out of focus pier feigned floatation on the distant waterline. All the while, an emotive storm of muddle and miscellany brewed inside me.

I miss you, Mum. As for Dad, I didn't know what to think.

Marcella explained that during the high season, the beaches laid packed, topless women included. How scandalous by my naïve British standards.

"The terraces fill quickly with tourists from all over the world. They adore our great Belgian beer," she said.

"Ah, and even the low-life English enjoy our scrumptious waffles with strawberries and fresh whipped cream," Dad said with an heir of nationalist pride. "Did you know Belgium has the best strawberries in Europe?"

He clearly loved his country. I found his patriotism amusing, knowing full well The Great British Empire ruled the waves, and soccer. As for beer, I didn't much care for the disgusting beverage that reminded me of Mum's demise.

"The snobby British know nothing of food, wine, and good beer. Tea, that's all they know," he cited, miming a cup in his hand with his pinky stuck up in the air and lips furrowed.

In the winter, life died here, Marcella informed us. Death is always sad. Without Mum *I* felt dead.

Supper came again.

I must ask the question. JP thinks it best to avoid the subject for now, but I need to know.

"Eh, excuse me, *Papa,* can you talk to me about Mum's last moments. How did she look?"

"She could barely talk when I saw her. I held her frail hand to comfort her. She took her last breath in front of me and made me promise to find you. I forgave her as she passed."

"Forgave her for what, if I may ask?"

"Because I didn't understood why she kept you from my love all these years, *Tonton*."

I didn't understand either. He continued.

"She hurt *you* more than me with her spite, my dear son."

"But, I don't understand why it took you so long to contact me, *Papa?*"

"What do you mean?

"Well, forgive me for asking, but why didn't she just give you my address or phone number before dying?"

Judging by the expression on his face, the question surprised him.

"Well, eh, it wasn't that simple, son. Eh, I mean, the hospital wouldn't give me her papers. They were quarantined and, as soon as I got them, I contacted you immediately."

But you said you were at her bedside before she passed away. If Mum's last wish was for us to be reunited, then why didn't she simply give you a phone number or an address? Why wasn't JP thinking the same thing?

Something seemed strange, very strange.

CHAPTER 25

Despite the misgivings and delights of Belgium, I expected to be back in rain-drenched London within days, as by order of the childcare authorities and the date on my return ticket. Besides, school waited, and a talent scout had recently approached me. He was setting up a trial with a top London soccer team called QPR. My dream was to play for the legendary Manchester United. I could see it already.

JP would return that evening. His obligations were to his wife, kids, and British Telecom. I counted down the hours and minutes before his departure, wanting him to stay longer, if not forever.

With his travel bag packed and a hint of trepidation on my part, we all climbed back into the lime-green van with Dad driving. He wore his officer's cap and silk scarf, just like when we first met. Mireille sat between him and Marcella in the front seat. I sat in the back with JP with nothing to say.

In Ostend, my brother and I exchanged the recently discovered cheek kisses to say good-bye. They felt awkward. He gave me a long-lasting hug and whispered in my ear.

"Take advantage of this chance, little brother, but be careful. I'm a phone call away if you need me."

His face revealed a hesitant expression as he disappeared through passport control. It added to the wave of angst that already warmed my forehead. I wanted to follow him back onto the ferry. But how bad could a day or two be without him in the land of chocolate and the best strawberries in Europe?

What if my father is still a child molester, though?

The long, lonely drive back to Blankenberge by the dunes without JP was loud and bumpy. The squeaks of the van wailed over the volume of the yowling engine. I wanted nothing but stillness and solitude to pull my thoughts together. There would be no soccer match for Salesian's that weekend and nothing to help me escape reality, other than Diavolino, who seemed to sense my emotional deficit.

Mireille sat next to me in the front. Dad drove. Marcella sat alone in the back. The kids were at school, and *Bobonne* probably waited by the window in her rocking chair, knitting.

I stared out my window in silence and watched the street stripes speed by. Dad and Marcella frequently disturbed my search for peace with questions and comments. I had no desire for idle chitchat, keeping my answers to yes and no, or pretending to not understand French. Mireille said nothing. She placed her hand on Dad's knee.

With each passing kilometer, I felt my brother's protection fade. The negative gut feeling only magnified my suspicions.

Why did Mum have to die? I wish Rudy were here.

I got accustomed to the van's loud noise. The white lines of the road became hypnotic and pacifying. The prospect of honoring Mum's dying desire filled me with pride. Here I was, reunited with my sister. I reached over and held her hand, relishing the thought of one day eating fish and chips with salt and vinegar with her (or ketchup). I'd teach her to speak English and drink tea with milk, too.

Deep down inside, however, the instinctual reservations as to whether she really could be my sister lurked.

Who's lying?

CHAPTER 26

My first weekend in this small town with a strange name began with Marcella announcing, "It's Friday! Bath night!"

"Yaayyyyyy!" shouted the kids.

Their excitement toward the more simple things in life brought such poetry to my troubled experiences.

"Can *Tonton* scrub our backs, *Papa*?" asked Christianne, the youngest and loudest.

Their enthusiasm tickled him. "*Oui*."

"I will be there in five," I said.

My forgotten French returned by the hour.

Fueled by glee, they bolted into the kitchen. I joined them. The kids splashed and sang songs in Flemish while I washed their hair. Their delight was contagious. Flemish did, indeed, sound like constipated cats with guttural complications.

I celebrated the moment with my own mirth. Suds flew everywhere.

They dried themselves and slipped into their pajamas. We headed to the living room to sip on hot chocolate.

"Can I sit on Tonton's lap?" asked one.

"No, it's my turn," demanded another.

"Then I'm gonna hold his hand!"

With too many palms in my hand, and bodies all over my lap, claustrophobia struck me. I pulled away to breathe, pushing them away.

Dad reacted. "What's wrong, *Tonton*?"

"*Rien*, nothing."

"Don't you love your brother and sisters?"

"*Mais bien sûr que oui*, yes, but of course."

"You know they are closer to you than Jean-Pierre and Rudy ever were, don't you?"

I disagreed with his remark, and made no comment, feeling guilty.

His eyes widened. "Mireille is your full-blood sister. Your black half brothers can't come before her, surely? Remember your mother's final wish before dying." He raised his shoulders. "You do love and respect your mother, don't you?"

How could I avoid betraying JP, Rudy, or Mum without offending anybody else?

"Yes, of course, I do, but--."

"No buts! So, who do you love more, Jean-Pierre and Rudy or Mireille, your full-blood sister?"

I stalled, in search of diplomacy.

"I love them all."

My failed tact offended him. He turned in despair to Mireille for understanding and sympathy.

She reached and grabbed his hand. "He needs more time, *coucou*."

The wrinkles on his forehead contracted. He sighed and paused. "You're right, Mireille. It's not your fault, son. My apologies."

What a relief!

He clapped his hands and rubbed his palms. "*Bon*, Mireille and *Tonton*, you can now take your bath together."

My shock must have been evident.

"Oh, it's normal to share the bath," he added.

Normal? There's nothing normal about that where I come from.

"You are family now and must act like the rest of your siblings without shame. Besides, we can't afford to run seven separate tubs."

Marcella and Mireille reaffirmed his statements as if programmed to do so. I pleaded. "But!"

"I said, no buts."

"But, I'd rather not. Please."

He bombarded me with persistence to the point of turning me into the family freak in the eyes of everybody else.

"What's wrong with Vital, Papa?" my siblings asked.

"Nothing," he replied. "He's not used to family life, that's all." He turned to Carol. "Were you ashamed to take a bath with your younger brother?"

"Of course not, *Papa*. We're a family. It's normal."

"You see, son, you are no longer an orphan living an abandoned life. Act like their big brother and not a stranger."

He expected too much too soon. This concept of kinfolk stressed me more than anything else. Maybe, family wasn't for me.

"Bedtime, children!" Dad yelled.

"Can *Tonton* tuck us in," asked Christianne in a voice filled with such innocence it melted my heart.

"*Mon plaisir*, my pleasure," I said with great reprieve, knowing the gesture would buy me time to plot an escape.

With pillows in place, lights out, and eyes shut, I painstakingly made my way back downstairs, dreading the dirty old bathtub. Once again, I attempted to avoid the encounter. My dislike fell on deaf ears. The weighty request turned into a command.

I watched the hot water run into the tub with horror, each gallon drowning my dignity. Mireille appeared more than comfortable to prepare for our first bath. She undressed in front of me revealing the naked body of a grown woman. I was mortified. She's bound to laugh at my body's puerility once nude. My pubic hair hadn't even shown signs of growth. Some staff members back at the home had joked about my physical immaturity, making me self-conscious and ashamed. I looked more like a twelve-year-old boy than a pubescent teen.

"Come on, don't be so shy, I'm your sister," Mireille said to encourage me.

She lowered herself into the water. "Hurry before the water gets cold." I cringed and blushed.

My clothes came off, stalling at each item, beginning with my sweater. I turned away and folded it meticulously before placing it on the stool. The sound of soft splashes susurrated behind me. I unbuttoned my shirt, unhurried, and laid it on top of the sweater. Next came my pants, sliding down my skinny legs to the chilled floor. Socks followed. My toes froze. Only my underwear remained. My heart raced. Panic kicked me in the gut. This felt so wrong and not normal, but the choice was not mine.

I took a deep breath and removed my underwear, doing everything to not expose myself.

How can I bathe with a girl, my alleged sister who I only met three days ago? It can't be right.

Mum! JP! I need you. God. What do I do? Stop acting like a self-conscious freak.

All my other siblings found it normal, so it had to be. Marcella backed up Dad's words, too. What did I know about family life?

She lathered my back, washed and rinsed my hair, scrubbed my arms, feet, and the rest of my body. I had only once seen a girl naked before—Mary, on the landing at the home. Never had one actually touched me. The sensation of Mireille's hands on my genitals caused a reaction. She appeared unaffected and simply continued. The shame and disgust plagued my morality like a locust invasion.

Why did Dad make me go through this? Why didn't I stand up for myself like a man?

Because I was not yet a man, but a shy little boy full of fear and no courage. Mum would be ashamed of me—I think. Or is this what she would have wanted, too?

The next morning at breakfast Dad suggested I stay longer than five days now that I had broken the ice and bonded with my sister so well.

The kids screamed with elation.

It was difficult to look anybody in the eyes and enjoy

the celebration. I felt so dirty from last night's soapy encounter.

"I need to go back to England; I have but four months left before graduation. Plus, the authorities will punish me."

"Family is more important than school *and* the authorities, *Tonton*. You must stay for your mum's and sister's sake."

"But I also need to go back for an upcoming soccer trial for a professional club."

"We have professional teams here, too. They are even better than over there."

Marcella and Mireille backed up his words again. He determined I would stay. My word once again counted for nothing. It was me against them. Diavolino seemed to be the only entity that related. I wanted to hide with him in the darkness of the cellar or run away, but not back to the home. So then, where?

CHAPTER 27

Dad showered me with objects of affection: clothing, jewelry, a stereo system, and a racing bicycle.

"Wow! I always dreamt of a bike like that, Dad. This will be the first one I haven't needed to scramble together with salvaged parts. It's spectacular. *Merci!*"

It had fancy center-pull breaks, professional slick tires, and even a sporty drinking bottle and holder.

Watch out Eddie Merckx.

The warm embrace of acceptance and answered prayers had finally found me, despite the "normal" family acts. A safety net other than sympathetic schoolteachers and supportive staff members appeared to be in place. I could now attempt to fly without a net, just like a fearless trapeze star. But I missed my friends at the home, bangers and mash with Oku, and apple crumble with custard from the kind dinner-ladies at Salesian's who often allowed me seconds.

Dad pressed me to contact the home and let them know of the change in plan. Sally thought it ill advised for me to stay longer without permission from the authorities, urging an immediate return.

"Just two weeks, Sally, that's all I need, please. I'm so happy to have this chance. I can catch up at school, no problem."

"Very well, but we will need to send your social worker to evaluate the situation," she said.

They'd need to determine if the house had a fire escape, hot running water, and were they feeding me? The typical bureaucratic crap I hated and was happy to be away from despite my concerns. I crossed my fingers in anticipation for the unknown, convincing myself all would end well, either way.

It will.

It will.

It will.

CHAPTER 28

My dad was awesome, and Belgian life seemed more promising than life back at the home. Not to mention, he enjoyed sports and had a great sense of humor. Better still, he liked soccer, my favorite sport in the world.

That week we watched a European Cup match on the telly between Anderlecht, a famous Belgian team, and an English team called Aston Villa. Mireille sat on his lap, as usual. I argued in favor of the British club, which annoyed him.

"You're Belgian. Enough of this Anglo-Saxon shit, son." He glanced over to Marcella, who remained neutral. "My son's a traitor! Send him to the guillotine."

When the British won by a single goal, his teasing tone changed drastically.

"Ugh, I detest that pompous phlegmatic island. They fucked me, they did, fucked me good and right up the ass. So did your mum. How can you support a team from that conniving little landmass?

I frowned, keeping my thoughts to myself. He stood up, pacing up and down, hands floundering about his head.

"They don't know the difference between shit and food. Boiled cabbage is considered fine cuisine for those toothless barbarians."

Marcella tried to calm him down.

"Shut up, woman, what do you know?"

Mireille stood up and hugged him. "*Papa, Cheri,* it's nothing."

He held her and kissed her forehead. "You're right. My son will learn to love his beautiful Belgium. He's just lost and confused, that's all. It's not his fault." He walked over, embraced me, patted my back and kissed me on the forehead. "It's not your fault, son. It's not your fault."

I wanted to push him away, but my well-mannered and submissive nature prevented me.

"There is so much for you to learn, *Tonton*. Life is not what it seems, you know. It's a circus chockfull of liars, pretenders, and manipulators." He sat down in his armchair. "Ugh, those British bastards!"

He immediately stood back up. His head visibly filled with pressure, his eyes with hate. I couldn't believe he was such a sore loser.

"Your mum thought me stupid when she fucked the police commissioner to have me arrested. I'm no clown. Your great-grandfather might have been a clown, but I sure to hell am not. CLOWN MY ASS!"

Almost twenty years had passed since my father talked of clowns. The sentiment still sat firm in my memory in 1999. But in stark contrast to his impression of clowns, the *Mystère* clown, Benny, seemed far from stupid. He was in fact, intelligent and wise. Many years later, and beyond my knowledge, I would meet the clowns in *Quidam*. A very different breed.

Like the cliché emotional description of clowns, Benny carried a sadness and aloneness I recognized. He showed no physical tears or a suitcase full of handkerchiefs, but his eyes reflected a dented soul. Like me, he played the social game well, but kept people at a distance.

Over the years at *Mystère*, he had offered advice, guidance, and insight on life, inner company politics and entertainment in general.

Many other things in the show brought me back to my childhood and youth, including its many characters and the meaning behind the show. The characters appeared to mirror my life.

Les Doubles Faces, that performed Chinese Poles with masks at the back of their heads', represented the individual who was in constant search of personal identity. I had yet to find my identity, though already thirty-five. The achievement of performing in Cirque helped add validation to my life.

A character in a beige costume that bore large teats, called *La Veche a Lait,* had the responsibility to protect and feed the three show babies. Safeguard and nurture had eluded me. The empty hole in me that only applause seemed to sedate felt like the abyss of the *Mystère* stage when lowered to minimum level. It lived as a dark, dangerous, bottomless pit to the naked eye. I always kept my dark crater hidden to the world, all the while acting on my stage—the stage that is life.

One of the many beauties of stage life, with its costumes and make-up, is that I could hide behind the mask they provided. I could flaunt my past shadows as a means of expression or interpretation without giving anything away.

When I rolled my head on the trapeze as a part of the choreography, nobody knew if that's how I actually felt, or if I was translating the music or the poetry of the act. Likewise, when I aggressively fisted the air during bungee, nobody knew if today's expression was anger, pride, joy, or revenge.

My past definitely fueled my expression. I had learned to use it to great advantage. The scars never fully healed, however.

Benny sat in the corner of the green room, puffing a cigarette, when the PA system announced the fifteen-minute countdown to show time. Chris and I played Ping-Pong, slamming balls, diving and hustling for each and every point. Neither of us enjoyed losing. I'd learned to play and develop a passion for the game back at the home when about eight. It remained as much an escape at Cirque as in my childhood.

Benny grumbled. "Shouldn't you be getting ready? When are you gonna' learn?"

"Never. There's still plenty of time," I responded and stalled the game.

"Today's youth, what a waste."

His costume was a white shirt veiled beneath an oversized black suit that concealed his skinny frame. His shoes were oversized, of course. He spiked and puffed his hair, making it look like a bomb had exploded in his face. A black ruffled tie completed the picture.

Benny's aged, powdered face stayed expressionless. He opened his jacket, placed his hand into the inside pocket, and pulled out something and fiddled. He showed me a red clown nose rested atop his extended middle finger. He gave a subtle smirk.

All other performers, mainly the Russians and Romanians, left the smoke-filled room to prepare for the second show.

"Have a good one," I said.

"Try to have one, too, V—if you make it in time."

He took one final, long-lasting drag of his cigarette and dabbed it into the ashtray and headed out. Chris and I continued hitting the Ping-Pong ball back and forth. It consumed us, and the minutes flew by unnoticed.

A final warning copied from the PA system. "Stand by, five minutes. Places please."

"Oh, shit," Chris whispered, tossing his paddle.

We weren't even in costume.

Both of us scrammed out the door, legging it through the narrow hallway down one flight of stairs to our dressing room. Chris almost knocked over a laundry lady coming the opposite direction.

Our dressing room sat empty.

"Dude, we're screwed," Chris said.

"Tell me about it! Crap, where's my headpiece?"

"Don't know, gotta' go. See ya'."

Sons-a-bitches, this is no time for a prank!

I found my headpiece on top of my locker and sprinted along the lengthy and obscure fourth floor hallway. It spanned the entire three hundred, or so, feet of backstage. I flew down the stairwell in a panic, passing another wardrobe lady returning from break.

"You're in trouble," she teased.

"No shit. Who cares? What, they're gonna fire me?"

I'd leave *Mystère* within weeks due to creative changes they were making. My last show would be on December 31, 1998. Five years and two thousand shows had passed too quickly.

I arrived backstage panting. The doors to the theatre were open. Performers had already entered the curtain of smoke that blanketed the entrance. Mitzy, another backstage manager, pointed to her watch, then the opening. I normally stood second in line. Today I entered last, taking extra large gallant strides to my usual spot in the aisle.

I observed the pageantry, still catching my breath from the long run. Sweat dripped down my forehead and lower back. Another show opening to add to the previous two thousand I had witnessed. Monotony had long since kicked in. My mind wandered off to a different type of circus—that of my father, life in the home and adolescence in general.

CHAPTER 29

The rapidly approaching appearance of my social worker freaked Dad out, who had no choice but to walk the tightrope across a void of uncertainty.

"What right do they have to invade my house and check up on me? Who could care more for his son than a father?"

"It's a stupid formality," I said. "It's no big deal. He'll be in and out in no time."

That morning JP called to check that all sat well. I told him about the social worker's arrival that afternoon.

"It'll be fine. Let him know what you want."

Dad stood listening. He always did, making the conversations uncomfortable.

"Listen, Jake, I'm just a phone call away if any funny stuff happens. Has he tried anything?"

I spoke with the thickest possible cockney accent just in case Dad still understood some English. I wasn't a stupid clown, either.

"Nah, course not. It's just… ah, it's nuffin'. Everyfing's kosher, mate."

"He's listening, isn't he?"

"Roger that, governor."

I wanted to tell him so many things. I needed to share that things seemed strange. It didn't make sense that Mireille always sat on his lap regardless of what she was wearing or not wearing. She kissed her father a lot. Her kisses sometimes became playful bites. She would even jokingly suck her father's lips and laugh when done too hard. He'd reciprocate.

I don't know if I kept silent out of fear, humiliation, or because the thought of finally finding love and family outweighed the peculiarity. I think it was a combination of everything.

When the call ended, Dad bombarded me with questions, wanting to know exactly what JP had said. I lied.

"Dad, why don't I go back to England, finish the last couple of months of school, then come back for good?"

"Is that your brother's idea?"

"No, of course not. I just want to finish school. Only four months to go, that's all."

"We'll sign you up at school here. There is nothing in England for you."

"But I don't speak Flemish."

"You must choose between family or the institution. You'll be on the streets when you turn eighteen if you go back. They don't give a damn about you. You're a faceless number. This is your home, forever!"

It was true they didn't give a damn.

He took his gold necklace off and placed it around my neck. I'd never had a gold necklace before.

"Well, what do you think, son? Take a look in the mirror. It suits you perfectly."

It looked spectacular! I positioned it beneath my shirt, held my hand against it and thanked him. He undid the top buttons, making his great gift viewable to the world. His face emitted pride. Confusion and fear crowded my thoughts.

CHAPTER 30

***Mystère's* overture ended** with the baby throwing his large, bouncy, red ball to the beige dressed character with teats. On cue, I sauntered back down the aisle and through the open steel doors to backstage.

Mitzy, dressed in all black, wearing a headset, approached me. "Why were you late?" she said with a gentle voice.

"I couldn't find my headpiece. Sorry."

"You know you'll need to go to the office after the show."

They might fire me yet.

A muscular Russian man with long curly hair appeared from that same abyss to replace the baby. His biceps bulged; his six-pack reflected the light beams.

I watched his act from the wings in admiration. I had learned some of his basic moves between shows in the training room. A contagious hunger to grow and improve always existed backstage. I loved the learning and self-challenging process Cirque instilled.

After crunches and push-ups before bungee trapeze, I changed costume and headed to the tech ring. Comments regarding my lateness continued.

"Someone's getting suspended, or fired," taunted Waldo, the retired boxer turned rigger from Chile.

"Ah, piss off," I replied with an appreciation for his humor.

"What time is it, Vital?" asked Benjamin, the lanky head-rigger, with a wry smile.

"Very funny, Benjamin."

He flashed his light at my harness to double-check my safety. "You're all set. Have a good one."

At the end of the act, Chris and I prepared for the finale climax. We stood motionless on our trapezes forty-five feet above and at opposite ends of the stage. The girls finished their closing routine—a sequence of incredibly fast aerial rotations we called "spin outs". I remember learning them back in Montreal during the eight-hour days of formation. They made me want to puke for the few first weeks.

The music shifted down a gear to a suspenseful mood. I nodded, giving Chris the standby. He signaled back. We locked gazes. *Let's do this!*

Peter, the tall, meticulous American juggler hiding up in the tech-ring, initiated our swing. He gave a gentle tug of a thin rope called a trick line. It attached halfway up our trapeze and led to him via a small pulley.

On the forward swing, I pushed hard onto the trapeze bar. This crucial first swing was the most important. It established synchronicity, lest I stop and do over and ruin the act. After several powerful thrusts, my swing took me within inches of the red circular contraption that posed as the centerpiece of the ceiling. A thick, reddish, textured fabric covered it. The director called it the Sun. When needed, The Sun opened and closed like an accordion, allowing for set changes.

On the final backswing, I nodded to Chris, indicating one more drive before take off. My momentum was so strong I partially disappeared into the slits of the Sun inches away from the unprotected wrought iron skeleton of the grid.

On the backswing, I dove. The momentum hurtled me in the opposite direction of Chris with such vigor I could have flown through the theatre walls out into the traffic on Spring Mountain Road.

The music stopped on cue, leaving a silent void. I was so close my body almost grazed the ceiling behind me. I could see the details of its rough surface as I soared. The sound of passing air whistled in my ears, cooling my forehead and chest. The strands of smiling seaweed on my costume quivered in the current, leaving a comet-like trail. The murmurs suggested spectators engulfed in a vortex of dramatic anticipation.

The bungees pulled hard and reached their maximum tension. They forced an extreme reverse of direction. I zipped toward my partner at lightning speed. The audience groaned, winced, and gasped. They didn't know if we were set to crash and pulverize each other.

Something could go seriously wrong at any given moment in this environment, other than colliding. A bungee could snap. A carabineer might fail. My harness could slip open. We ignored the danger and fear. Each terrifying option would release me to the mercy of the stage. The fall would probably take my life, if not break every bone in my body and that of others seated below in the wake of the crash landing.

We flew horizontal like superheroes, arms out sideways from our shoulders. I watched my partner get closer by the half second. I waited till the final perilous moment before reacting. The audience gulped. They sucked the remaining air out of the theatre. Yards turned to feet, feet to inches. I observed the details of Chris' make up. Drops of sweat speckled his dark, chocolate skin. He had blended his white highlights well. They accentuated his cheekbones, jaw, and chin.

You missed your eyebrows.

Just as our faces were about to kiss, the audience cringed.

We arched our backs. Our chests smacked against each other emitting a loud flat slap of a sound. Chris' broad muscular body weighed a lot more than mine, so the collision winded me. The rebound, combined with the tug from the bungees, thrust me forcefully back to the other side of the theatre.

Maintaining control, I initiated and completed a slow back lay out, spying the audience. Some clenched their seats. Others viewed with amazement splattered on their faces.

I yanked the cords, contracted my stomach. I pulled my knees firmly into my chest to form the smallest possible ball and rotated forward. I opened my body at the perfectly timed moment. Chris' arms extended toward me, palms up. A split second offered the opportunity to grab his wrists. I held them tight. The tension of the cords tried to rip us apart.

We hovered smack in the middle of the space between low and high like a UFO insulting the laws of physics. The audience yelled.

Chris smiled and said, "Glad you could make it; heard you were running late."

"I was. Gotta go!"

I released the grip and zoomed backward. At the bottom of the bungee stretch, I pulled the cords with all my might and zipped back up to sit on the trapeze in one powerful swoop. My hamstrings crushed against the bar sending a current to my toes. The act ended. The bungee team turned to the audience and bowed by poetically grabbing the air with our fist, the signature salute of *Mystère*.

That sound of applause was my drug. I felt high, addicted, and loved. Adrenaline pumped through my veins. My heart raced. The safety cable came down and lofted me upward.

Waldo came over to assist me. "That was a close one. Break any ribs today?"

"Better check with Chris."

"Hey, it's Sunday, drinks and sushi tonight?" he asked.

"No, I have school in the morning."

"It's too late to get brains, V."

"Still gonna' try. Have a good weekend, bro."

I grabbed the usual bag of ice from physio for my shoulder and signed up for tomorrow's treatment. The pain seemed to never go away. I soldiered on. We all did. There was no other choice, lest risk losing our job.

Once iced and cooled down, I changed into *Pagne,* a greenish brown tight spandex costume with one leg and no top. A latex bald cap with anemic strands of hair and rubber finished the primitive tribal look.

I'd usually head to the training room and practice other disciplines, such as Chinese poles and trampoline, or do weights. Today, I went back to the smoke-filled green room for some more Ping-Pong.

The Russians and Romanians, also wearing *Pagne,* played dominoes. They smoked their final cigarettes before high bar. Some called their wives on the payphone.

I never understood how they could smoke so heavily, not to mention the Vodka, and still perform at such high levels. It took all sorts to make up this international cast of elite artists, each with their own quirks, rituals, and habits.

Dominoes reminded me of Europe for some unknown reason, but I never played. Nostalgia always lingered. It invaded my present whenever it pleased. One day I would escape my past and live for tomorrow, if not in the now.

I had come a long way since the loveless days at Howard's Lane and the life-changing years with Dad when life was a very different type of circus.

Agatha Christie once said, "I learned that one can never go back, that one should not ever try to go back—that the essence of life is going forward. Life is really a one way street."

Forward I must walk until my demons are no more. The past can only serve me as a reminder of where I started. I cannot be its prisoner forever.

Fear will not be my master.

CHAPTER 31

The hours before the caseworker's arrival were tense. His evaluation would determine my future. Dad was anxious.

"Make it clear to him you want to stay, *Tonton!* You do want to stay, don't you?"

"Yes, but…."

"But what, I thought we were clear. You're staying to honor your mum's last wish and be with your sister, aren't you?"

His words always had such finality, leaving no room for debate.

The caseworker arrived. He didn't speak French, and Dad no English. I translated the limited exchange. More importantly, the house had a fire escape and heat. I also had new shoes and a sparkly gold chain to show how wonderful life was in Belgium. Conclusion: permission to stay a couple of extra months granted!

The social worker shook my dad's hand. I accompanied him to the front door. The family trailed behind.

He turned to me. "We are only a phone call away should you change your mind, Vital. Congratulations! I'm sure you will be happy with your new family. Good luck."

With his work done, the caseworker ferried his way back across the Channel into the bureaucratic office drizzle of theories and statistics I so disliked.

I couldn't help but wonder if I'd made the right choice. That horrible gut feeling dawdled, yet again.

The day after the social worker left, I missed the home and Mum more than ever.

"Can we visit Mum's grave, please?" I asked.

"*Bien sûr, mon filston,* of course, my little son."

He drove me to Brussels, an hour away. As always, Mireille sat next to him with her hand on his lap, and Marcella alone in the back.

We walked through the cemetery along tarmac pathways, passing fresh laid graves, longstanding gothic tombstones, and soon to be used lots. It reeked of loss; mordant tears dried by handkerchiefs and buried memories.

Mum's greyish, pale blue, freckled granite tombstone lay somber. Only withered pink perennials and a dull, insipid sky kept it company, emphasizing her lonely demise. "REGINE TSHILUMBA 1942-1981" lay embossed in bronze lettering beneath a thin, elegant cross.

Thirty-nine was too young to die. Sixteen was too young to lose a mum.

It struck me hard to realize she rested only six feet below in the wintry earth. I tried to imagine her radiance. Instead, the disturbing vision of a decaying body and a flimsy skeleton with scraggly hair and exposed teeth raped my thoughts. I wanted to run.

Dad placed his arm around my shoulders. "We'll give you a moment alone. Take your time."

At first, I had nothing to say, staring at her name in defeat. I reminded myself she would want me to stand tall and dignified. I inhaled, clasped my hands, closed my eyes, and bowed my head.

Dear Mum, sorry for not being there to comfort you in death. May God's guiding light shine upon your soul for eternity. I will make you proud one day, I promise. Amen.

I couldn't figure out why Dad had been so honorable, considering he hated Mum for what she had done to me and to him. The feeling that something was off kilter prickled my stomach—again. I didn't yet have the experience to listen to those gut warnings sent by the soul.

The Jacob family circus had only just begun.

Even if I had listened, I was still too afraid and childlike, though sixteen, to stand up for my convictions.

Mum will never be proud. I'm such a pansy.

The subject of Mum's grave became a forbidden topic. He never took me again. I didn't fight for her. I abandoned and forsook her to eternal solitude.

When will I grow up, say goodbye to Tonton, and stop being so submissive?

CHAPTER 32

Dad enrolled me at school as promised. Most of the pupils shared that they'd never actually seen a person of color in real life, other than my sister and two half-caste boys who lived in this town of only fifteen thousand inhabitants.

Here, they called blacks niggers.

If it's not skinheads and the racist National Front party, it's narrow-minded honkies from a Belgian coastal hamlet. Never seen a black person before? That's bloody ridiculous.

"Dad, I want to go back to England. They don't like blacks here. They've never even seen one before."

"I will drop you off and pick you up from school tomorrow. When they see your father is white, it will make you more acceptable. They won't see you as a dirty nigger."

Though the word nigger was less offensive, if not common in French and Dutch, it remained a piercing insult. The fact my father used the term with such ease only magnified the tarnish.

You're insulting me, my brothers, and my mum – your ex wife.

It didn't make sense.

Many pupils stared from a safe distance, others stepped right up for a closer look without reservation. I felt like a circus novelty act. I turned the initial discomfort of attention to my personal enjoyment, perhaps a defining moment—this was my first audience, my first taste of the spotlight. Being different had its perks.

"We don't like niggers, but you're okay. You're not like them," they said.

Is that a compliment or an insult? I'm confused.

Nothing, other than chocolate and waffles, made sense in Belgium. Nonetheless, Dad's theory proved right. They accepted me and didn't view me as a dirty nigger. I made many new friends.

Merci, Papa.

Above and beyond the race challenge, I went from my fifth and final year at Salesian's as a sixteen-year-old, to the second form with eleven and twelve-year-old Flemish kids. I hated that relegation even more than the word nigger.

Crap, I'll be twenty before I ever graduate. If only Dad would let me go back to England to finish my last couple of months.

Nearly everybody at school spoke some English. Most were more than happy to practice it with me. Even the teachers made the effort to translate parts of class. I'd otherwise sit, listen, drift into daydream, and question the strange guttural sounds they called Flemish.

Dad set up a trial for the local soccer team. They played in a semi-professional provincial league. Though shorter, thinner (and darker) than all the other players, I made an impression. They immediately signed me up to the Under 21s, or *junioren.*

I might play for Manchester United, yet.

That very weekend I played my first match, wearing the new Adidas Santiago soccer shoes Dad had bought. I even scored a goal. My ecstatic teammates rubbed my hair and hoisted me into the air.

Don't touch my Afro!

We won the match. The coach congratulated me, "Bravo, welcome to *Sport Blankenberge.*"

The local fans showed love. Belgium wasn't so bad. I could live with being a half nigger everybody liked. I needed nothing more in life than soccer, really. While on the pitch, the world took care of itself. The ball, as it had always done, negated all concern for tomorrow. Yesterday's sadness and today's regrets disappeared at each kick.

I am happy. Dad is proud. We're a team.

CHAPTER 33

Bathing with Mireille became a weekly occurrence. She taught me how to lather her body and continued to wash mine with a hand cloth. It remained embarrassing, but I had no choice but to accept the situation as the norm. Dad pounded home his rhetoric with a Hitler-like conviction. Wash, rinse, repeat, and repeat again until subject complies and salivates at the bell.

Marcella and Mireille voluntarily backed up his words on cue.

"It's normal!" they said.

Grandma remained quiet. She'd only nod to affirm, if and when her son asked her a direct question.

Sleeping assignments changed again at Dad's request. Mireille and I now shared the large single bed. To make matters creepier still, she slept naked at night. I lamented. It made no difference. Wash, rinse, and repeat.

"Christophe has always shared a bed with his sisters," Dad stated. "Why wouldn't you do the same, *Tonton*?"

Jeanine, the eldest after Mireille, upheld his words, too. "It's normal to sleep in the same bed, Papa. We're family. We love each other."

"You see, son, it's all about love. Love, something you've never experienced. It's normal family life. I would never hurt you. Never."

It MUST be normal if EVERYBODY is saying it, even the children. What do I know about family? Nothing!

I complied and pooled in the same bed next to Mireille's naked body. I assumed the long, repeated goodnight kisses she gave on the lips were sisterly gestures of affection.

I tried one more time to express my discomfort.

"Dad, it feels strange to sleep and bathe with Mireille."

"Giving kisses on the cheek to say hello also felt strange a few weeks ago, right?"

He had a point. Silly me. I just needed to adapt. I was no longer an orphan and should embrace family life. Every family probably did this.

You finally have family, so stop fighting it. What a complete and utter bloody tit you are, V.

The next day at lunch Dad sat at the head of the table as always. Everybody had assigned seating by order of importance as if in a boardroom meeting. Mireille sat to his right and me to his left. Marcella sat at the opposite end next to Grandma. The flowery plastic table cover lay cluttered with mustard, mayonnaise, tasty, fresh, white bread, and disgusting cold cuts like raw, minced meat and jellied pig brain.

Dad asked what my experiences were with the opposite sex. It seemed like a strange topic to have in front of children and Grandma. He repeated the question, reminding me to not be shy in front of family. "There is nothing to hide here."

"I've never had a girlfriend," I told him, with so much embarrassment my palms got sweaty and my cheeks warm.

His face lit up in amazement. "What! Never? I'd seduced several women by the time I was your age. I can't believe it, my son's as good as a eunuch."

His comments amused everybody. Even Grandma cracked a smile.

A eunuch?

He was right. I'd never looked at women as objects of lust, rather nurturers. Not to mention, I was physically immature and ashamed of my body. I would have never shared it with the opposite sex. I'd noticed at Salesian's during P.E. showers, that I was the only boy without genital fuzz. Besides, girls scared me. Give me a soccer ball over a girl any day.

"Have you ever kissed a girl?" he asked.

"Of course."

"How many times?"

I kept quiet, knowing it had only ever happened once. I slobbered the kiss and made a fool of myself, wishing it never actually happened.

He looked over to my little brother.

"Even Christophe has kissed a girl. Right, son?"

A huge grin appeared on Christophe's proud face.

"Many. I have two girlfriends at school."

"That's my boy!" Dad said, extending his right palm toward my little brother. Dad took a last sip of coffee, signaling to Marcella for a refill. "Okay, listen. We have to make you a man, *Tonton*."

The thought sounded exciting. The chat continued that evening when everybody had gone to bed. Marcella and Mireille remained.

"Have you ever even touched a woman?"

I lied.

"Of course."

I wanted him to think me a man already. I hated being the sweet, innocent, and pure British outcast of the Jacob family.

"When I say touch, I mean, you know…touch with your finger. Pleasured till she says stop—stimulated back."

I didn't have the guts to answer. He went on.

"In Africa, a boy is sent out into the wilderness with an auntie, niece, or any other woman who is a part of, or very close to, the family. They will teach him about manly responsibilities and sexuality."

His aunties had allegedly done it for him, granted, not in the African wilderness. My mum had apparently done it for her cousins, and so on, and so on. He labeled this, *l'education sexuelle*.

According to him, and under the given circumstances, the job was Marcella's, his wife. He suggested I call her *Marraine* (stepmother or godmother).

The ways of manhood under his plan seemed a little perverse. Marcella and Mireille qualified his words. Wash, rinse, and repeat! I believed them.

"I love you, son, and want to help you become a man."

Marcella commented, too. "We all love you and want to help you. I understand if you're not comfortable yet, but I'm more than happy to help."

Grandma said nothing. I wondered what she thought. Did she know something I didn't?

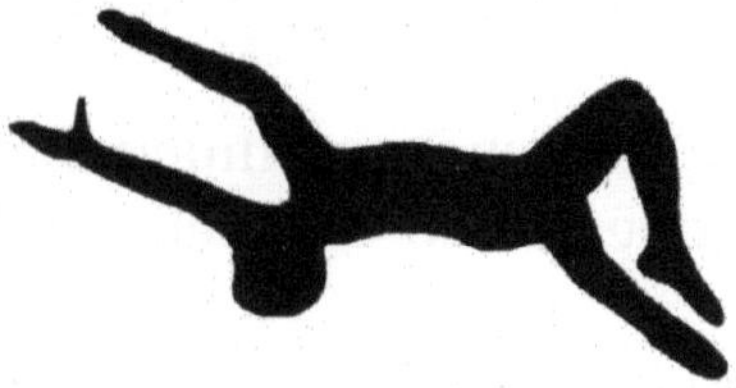

CHAPTER 34

The next day was more of the same—talk of *l'education sexuelle.*

The chat between Dad, Mireille, and I took me by surprise. He made the weirdest request out of nowhere. "Take off your top, Mireille."

She did, willingly, without hesitation, revealing her braless breasts. I looked down and away.

"What, they're not beautiful enough for you to look at?" he asked. "Do you want to become a man or not?"

I nodded.

"Then you can't be afraid to look at a woman. When I was your age, I had already slept with plenty of women," he bragged again."How many women have you slept with?"

Mireille giggled. I lied.

"One."

"Who?"

"Um, my friend's sister back in England."

Another lie.

"How many times?" Dad asked.

"Eh, I don't know. Um, several times. I...I didn't count."

I knew he could see through my fibs. He took a step closer to Mireille. Almost standing next to her, his hands gestured toward her chest.

"Look! Aren't they just beautiful?"

He appeared proud of her. By the illustration on her face, his pride made her happy. I, too, wanted him to be proud of me. I wanted him to think I was as cool as he was.

"Your sister is only fourteen, but I already see grown men crave her chest. That's what real men do, son, they lust after women. You do like women, don't you?" He allowed no time to answer. "A real man's purpose is to fornicate. It's the law of nature." The words flowed relentlessly from his mouth. "You better not be a dirty faggot." He raised his voice. "Are you a dirty faggot?"

"Of course not."

"Then how can you resist looking at naked breasts? Look at how firm they are."

I raised my gaze.

"They're not like the breasts of nigger women. Your mum's breasts were typical for an African. They hung flat like rolled out French bread dough down to her waist."

That comment stabbed my heart, my dignity, and my mum's honor. I felt only pain, no anger. He continued.

"Mireille is lucky to have European breasts. Go on, feel how firm they are. Go on, don't be afraid."

I was not only afraid, I was shocked and repulsed.

"You do find your sister's breasts beautiful, don't you?"

I had nothing to say.

"Well, don't you?"

The words could not leave my lips.

"So, you're rejecting your sister? How can you hurt your sister's feelings like that?"

"I'm not. It's just that...."

"Then tell her you find her breasts beautiful."

I gave him the answer he pressured me for, wanting to spit and rinse my mouth out.

"If you think they're beautiful, why wouldn't you want to touch them?"

"I don't know," I mumbled.

"Speak up!"

"It feels wrong. I can't do it."

"What! Feels wrong? You think it's wrong to become a man?"

I shrugged my shoulders and eyed the floor in shame.

"Touch and feel how firm they are if you want to become a man!"

My mind surrendered, but my hands refused. An empty silence filled the room. I caught my breath, experiencing each exhale to the fullest. The tic of the grandfather clock deafened me.

His tone changed. He spoke softly with amplified tenderness. "Look at me, my dear son. I love you."

He waited as if expecting me to reciprocate the sentiment. I remained still.

"I want to help you, my dearest Tonton. There is nothing to be ashamed of. They're only breasts."

He took a step closer and cupped her right breast in his palm. Mireille smiled. I watched his fingers sink in and out of her flesh.

"See, it's okay. They won't bite."

I can't believe my father just groped my sister's tits.

I froze. A debate flared in my head. Should I or not? Could I?

Dear God, please give me the strength to become a man and make Dad proud of me, too.

I couldn't. I failed my dad.

He continued the topic for a while. At each of his regurgitated phrases, I believed a little more that her chest wouldn't bite, and that it was the right path to manhood.

That night in bed I placed my hand on Mireille's naked chest. I bit the apple and gently sunk my fingers into her flesh. I felt both pleasure and revulsion.

Our Father Who art in heaven….

As usual, God seemed uninterested in my prayers.

Why pray, anyway? Religion's stupid. It's all hypocritical nonsense. The Lord is obviously not MY bloody shepherd.

The only person who might have listened was JP,

but Dad didn't allow me to make long distance calls. Besides, JP hadn't called in over a month. Dad rubbed in that very fact.

"Why doesn't your brother call any more, *Tonton*? I think he's jealous of you."

Why have you abandoned me, too, John?

"How can you love your brother when he's turned his back on you?"

John, you bleedin' prat. I hate you.

"If I were you, *filston*, little son, I'd burn all of his pictures and never speak to him again."

I considered the proposition. Dad was right. My brother didn't deserve the honor I gave him.

Diavolino, my four-legged, red-haired friend listened. He could not offer advice, however.

Hail Mary, full of Grace.... How can there be a God when there are wars and mother's die too soon. If God existed, He wouldn't torture me like this. What did I do to deserve this? Answer me, God! I hate you, too!

This was maybe the third time in my life I truly felt anger and hate. The first, when the social workers tried to send me to a foster home without my brothers. The second, when the warden ignored my request to allow the "black is beautiful" Comfort from the home to accompany me on the first day of school. Maybe worse than hating other people and God, I hated myself for having bit the apple.

I'm a sick and twisted bastard. No, you're not! Don't be stupid. L'education sexuelle is normal. Everybody does it. I just need to get used to this family crap – Holy Mary, Mother of God....

It must be right. Dad will be proud of me. A boy goes out into the wilderness and is taught the ways of manhood – an auntie, a sister – l'education sexuelle. No, I am bloody sick. No, it's l'education sexuelle. L'education sexuelle. L'education sexuelle. It must be right. They ALL said so, even Grandma. It IS right – Fuck!

I hated the Virgin Mary, too. As for the Holy Ghost, He could piss off.

CHAPTER 35

The wash, rinse, and repeat cycle continued for the next months, extending beyond *l'education sexuelle*. Dad's anti-British sentiment also never ceased to aggress me. He gradually blotted out everything I knew, loved, and believed in.

"I forbid you to display pictures of Jean-Pierre, Rudy, *and* your mum. People here will think you're racist and will dislike you for it. You're neither an Englishman nor a nigger, so stop associating with them."

I still couldn't understand why he was such a bigot. The more he rejected and dissolved my emotional ties, the more I felt degraded and voiceless. The little roots I owned, he slowly severed like Mr. Aim's did to Kunta Kinte. I felt afraid and helpless, like a runaway slave desperate for freedom. He broke me with words. I gave in and denied everything I was.

Yes, massah. Weez don't be talkin' to no niggas like JPs and Rudies no mo'. Weez be hatin' on those English folk, too, yes sir.

I took down all pictures and turned my back on England, my brothers, and Mum. I became Toby. Dad owned me.

I needed to escape or find other options. I learned from Debbie back at the home that drugs or suicide were an option. In the meantime, the attic rooms could offer refuge.

"Can I use the attic rooms, Dad? They're so cool. You promised I could when I first arrived, remember. I did have my own room back at the home, you know. I am, after all, sixteen."

"Very well."

What a relief. Partial escape. No more sharing the single bed with Mireille. No more sexual education. It offended Mireille. She stopped talking to me. Dad demonstrated grave indifference toward me as a result of having rejected his favorite daughter—the only daughter who always sat next to him at the dining table, and in the car—the only daughter for whom he reserved a spot next to him to hold his hand during walks along the promenade—the only daughter he took baths with and slept next to in bed—the only daughter who sucked his lips as an apparent joke—the only daughter who allowed him to fondle her bare breasts and sit naked on his lap to watch TV.

My soul cried. My heart bled at the rejection. Not even soccer provided enough redemption to make the world okay. The clouds lost their silver lining. Rain poured. The sky turned black.

All my other siblings showed me their indifference by default of their father's example. Carole, the third youngest after Mireille, was the exception. She secretly winked to let me know she was on my side. She even sneaked up to my room for five seconds to say, "*Je t'aime, grand frère,* I love you, big brother."

Carole had a different mind set than the others, which made her a victim. She even looked different. Her dark-blonde hair lay thinner, and her freckles were more pronounced. She had a nasty scar from a playful dog bite running across her cheek and thick lips. Her large teeth protruded. Dad never called her beautiful. She knew she was the least attractive of the children.

As the most athletically talented and opinionated of the gang, Dad treated Carole with exaggerated discipline, frequently yelling at her. She withdrew into a quiet, ugly duckling afraid to quack. Regardless of who he yelled at, the house trembled. Even Grandma shuddered.

Marcella oftentimes came up to my room, too, in secret. She risked castigation. "I can only stay a minute or two, but I want you to know I am here for you."

She demonstrated great affection and understanding, especially during the morning wake-up calls while Dad slept. She would lie on my bed to hug me and make me feel less isolated and abandoned.

"Your father loves you; he just has a strange way of showing it, *Tonton*."

"He doesn't love me. If he did he wouldn't deprive me of everything I know and love."

"He just wants you to let go of your past. You need to forget yesterday to enjoy your new family."

"Jean-Pierre, Mum, and Rudy are not my past. They never will be, and he'll never take them away from me."

"Ah, *Tonton*. My poor *Tonton*."

I didn't want sympathy. I wanted understanding, freedom to love, to be loved, and to be myself.

Marcella held me tighter still. She caressed my face and repeatedly kissed me on the cheek and forehead. The affection helped me face the day, knowing somebody cared, but the rejection from my sister hurt too much. Mum's spirit lived on through her.

That weekend I knocked at Mireille's door at a rare moment when she wasn't sitting naked on our father's lap.

"I'm sorry," I said. "I didn't mean to reject you. Mum wouldn't want us to ignore each other. Please, forgive me."

I slept in her bed that night and *l'education sexuelle* continued, until the uneasiness once again escalated beyond insanity and I rejected her. She stopped talking to me. Wash, rinse, and repeat!

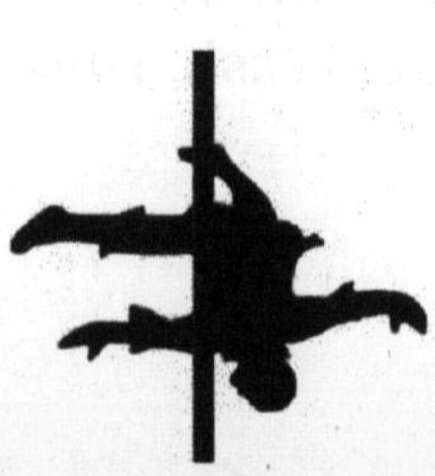

CHAPTER 36

The weeks passed. Today's interactions mirrored yesterday's. Dad pounded more racist rhetoric down my throat, imposing his surprising political and moral views.

"Hitler was a misunderstood hero," he said with a smug expression. "If he had succeeded, we wouldn't have niggers and dirty Moroccans sully the streets of Brussels."

Did he not realize I was half black? It didn't make sense. I politely contradicted his opinion. He erupted.

"What do you know? Have you ever lived in Brussels?"

"No." I looked down to the floor. "I've only been there once to visit Mum's grave, remember."

"Son, you haven't the slightest idea what you're talking about. I only left Brussels to live with these Flemish peasants because of the stabbings and filth. The city stinks. Hitler would have gassed them and eliminated the problem."

I couldn't rap my brain around the fact my dad was a Nazi supporter. I listened to the rest of his rant, trembling.

"Belgium is soft. We pay for the education of dirty foreigners, and they live off our welfare paid for by us Belgian's who have the damned decency to actually work."

What? You're criticizing welfare? If my history classes serve me correctly, Hitler created the welfare state, albeit a racist-totalitarian one. Besides, you haven't worked a day since I arrived.

"Send them back to their poor little countries and stop them raping our women. Dirty mackacks. Tell me I'm wrong!" His order made me stand at attention.

Why did he marry Mum; she was black? It doesn't make sense.

"Well! Am I wrong?" he thundered.

My voice reflected the fear he had instilled; yet I spoke my mind. "Sorry, but I'm, I'm not sure I can agree. I, em, I don't think there's anything Hitler did that is misunderstood or heroic."

He hollered and cursed for the next ten minutes. Spittle flew from his mouth. Rage bulged from his eyes, and Swastika's steamed out his ears as if he had channeled a fuming Fuhrer from the grave.

"You dare challenge me, son?"

My head shook no, but my mind shouted, *Yes, I do challenge you*. I'd already said too much.

"I forbid you to use the white racing bike. It can only be ridden by respectable children, that of which you're not! You're a nigger lover. If only you knew the truth about Africans."

He repossessed all the other gifts he had earlier bribed me with as punishment for taking off the sheepskin clothing I had learned to carry on my shoulders.

"You will understand one day, *Tonton*."

I could never understand his reasoning, let alone want to. To this day, I still lack comprehension. Besides, I didn't need his gifts. I silently cursed his birth and beliefs, wanting to shove his white racing bike up his white racist backside.

"Your pocket money is suspended, too," he added. "Now, go to your room."

My pleasure.

"What about soccer?" I asked.

"You can still go, but on foot."

In my mind, I clicked my heels, about turned, and goose-stepped out of the living room with my fingers across my upper lip. In reality, I hung my head and slithered out, gently shutting the door in defeat.

"I'll allow you to come down and eat!" he yelled through the door.

The stairs squeaked extra loud during the never-ending walk up to doom. The walls of my room narrowed and suffocated me. I lay dejected on the bed staring at the slanted ceiling. Even my escapist world of dream could not be visualized. Maybe I could channel Anne Frank and gain some strength and insight. The room darkened as evening set in.

"It's suppertime!" yelled Marcella from below.

I took a deep breath and traipsed down the four flights. The food was tasteless—the ambiance bitter.

"*Bon appetite,*" they all wished each other. I had no appetite.

Dad talked and laughed with his children. I chewed, drank, and swallowed, waiting for suppertime to end. Grandma nibbled in silence like a pigeon. Marcella accommodated everybody's drinking needs, in particular Dad's.

With a cramped stomach, I carried my cross back up the four flights of stairs into stillness and emptiness. I knew he would break me. He knew he would break me.

I walked to school the next day and everywhere else around town. The radio-cassette player he had given me went to Mireille, as did the portable television. The silence became too loud. Only the sound of isolation resonated off the grey, uneven walls.

"I am sorry, Papa."

Another battle lost for me. His truths became my truths.

Oui, Papa. Oui, Papa. Oui, Papa.

His words became mine.

Hitler should have gassed them. Niggers are, indeed, inferior – and smelly. North Africans are scum.

I'd neither met any Turks, Moroccans, or Arabs, nor had they done me any harm, but I disliked them. I hated JP. I forgot about Rudy and murdered all memories of

Mum. I didn't know who I was anymore, other than an unloved, lost, isolated kid.

Love? Love doesn't exist. It's a fairytale with hornless unicorns.

I knocked at Mireille's door that night begging for acceptance. She opened it and let me in. The visit aggravated my unrest. Yes, no, do, don't, why? Who's wrong? What's right? This isn't!

In desperation, I reached out to Marcella for advice. I now called her *Marraine* (Godmother). She extended even more understanding and affection. Her morning hugs in my bed became longer and tighter. She pressed her hips snug against my pelvis through the covers. Her kisses became more tender.

"I understand, *Tonton,* if you can't handle Mireille teaching you anymore," she whispered. "I am more than happy to help you, if it will make it easier for you." She pulled my head against her chest, stroking my hair. "It was your father's original plan, anyway."

"I just want to go back to England. I can't go on like this, *Marraine.*"

"Oh, *Tonton,* my dear *Tonton.*"

I fought back the sorrow, but the tears leaked down my cheek.

She joined me under the covers and held me close.

"There's nothing to be afraid of. I'll talk to your father. He's proud of the steps you've taken."

"What do you mean?"

"You don't know? Mireille tells him everything."

That added to my despair.

"No need to worry. I'm here for you. Tea or coffee this morning?" she asked with a bright smile.

"Tea, please."

The next morning she woke me up a little earlier than normal. She slipped under the covers again, holding me tighter and longer – and again the next morning – and the morning after that.

"Don't worry, I've spoken about it with your dad. He just wants you to become a man. It'll get him off your back." She kissed me on the lips and smiled caringly. "He'll show you love again if you become a man."

Please, just get him off my back. It's about to break, along with my heart and sanity.

"Relax, *Tonton*. Let me help you. Close your eyes and relax."

I did."

CHAPTER 37

By the time my first Belgian summer arrived, I realized that my father was not the only racist in this small Flemish coastal town, if not the entire country. But nobody came close to his extremism. My lost education troubled me more than the prejudice. Names had never hurt me. Insufficient schooling could!

I would have graduated by now, had I only stayed in London.

Two years of sixth form at Salesian's would have awaited me (equivalent to college). Law, Journalism, or P.E. sparked my interests.

I wonder how Oku did in his finals? Wish I knew how to contact him. I miss Howard's Lane.

Nobody there probably remembered me, anyway. Or, they'd all left and been replaced by a new generation of social rejects. The authorities had likely discarded my file. I'd become the forgotten statistic doomed to failure that I so feared. There was no going back. I was stuck in this new and very different country that disliked blacks, coloreds, niggers, and golliwogs even more than the UK.

Don't they all know Jesus is black?

The small town of Blankenberge came to life with each tourist that packed the summer streets. Restaurants and tearooms thrived. Terraces filled with patrons from all corners of The Benelux and Germany, sipping on cappuccinos or famous Belgian beer. Others scarfed down waffles and pancakes with whipped cream or sugar. Blankenberge turned into a mini working-class metropolis.

Nightlife and the many discotheques ignited my curiosity. I'd heard the soccer players and their girlfriends rave about one discotheque in particular, The Gin.

A tall, thin bouncer with long curly hair guarded the doorway of The Gin. He wore a black leather bomber jacket, tight, narrow jeans, and black biker boots. People went in and out the swinging doors freely. Loud music spilled onto the street. At sixteen I was old enough to enter. Time to discover.

"It's a private club, you can't come in," the bouncer said to me in a crude local dialect, placing his palm against my chest.

"But what about them?" I asked, pointing to a white couple entering without any hassle.

"Members only," he said, cupping his hand by his face to light a cigarette in the wind.

"What do you mean?"

Another group of whites walked past me and entered. He asked no questions, but simply wished them a pleasant night and not to forget his tip on the way out.

"What about them?" I demanded.

"It's a private club. Step away."

"I know they're not members."

"Step away now if you don't want trouble, you little, black midget."

I stepped away and walked across the Casino Square to another disco, The Beatles. Same story!

I went home dejected and shared the incident with Dad. The next day, he and Mireille accompanied me to The Gin. Dad spoke with the bouncer. Mireille translated from French to Flemish.

"Excuse me, young man, this boy is my son. Why can't he go in?"

The bouncer explained that they didn't let in Arabs or blacks because they caused too many fights.

"My son's not black, he's Mulatto," Dad explained to the doorman. "He's Belgian like you—like me. I'm his father and white, so he's equal to us both. Besides, he's a good lad and won't cause trouble."

The bouncer let me in. Dad told me to give the doorman a tip on the way out and thank him.

"Okay. Merci, Papa."

I can't believe they turned me down cause I'm black.

Behind the swinging doors waited a narrow passage that turned immediately right. A pinball machine stood at the end in the corner. Next to it rested a Space Invaders game. A group of guys holding half-full Stella Artois glasses and Carlsberg bottles surrounded it. To the left stood the opening to the bar and dance floor.

A waiter stopped me.

"The doorman said I could come in," I yelled.

He shrugged his shoulders, demanding I order a drink. The music pumped the beats so hard my heart pounded to the rhythm. I barely heard him. He pantomimed a drink. I ordered a coke.

"Fifty francs," he yelled.

Dad had not docked my pocket money that week, so I had a hundred francs in my wallet. The waiter turned to the bartender and shouted. In a flash, he handed me an elegantly curved glass bottle of chilled Coca-Cola. I paid him.

The excess cigarette smoke choked my lungs. Lights flashed and twirled. People laughed and drank at the bar. Some glanced over, making me feel like an intruder. I ventured further into the dim belly of the discotheque. Couples snogged on the obscured benches. Others seemed sound asleep or in a dream state. What a different world.

For a couple of hours, I observed, stood, and danced. The muscle of the music booming through the speakers consumed me. I grooved and forgot.

I tipped the bouncer twenty Belgian francs on the way out, dreading the walk home. Dad waited. It would be hell.

He welcomed me home with two cheek kisses. "So, how was it?"

"Pretty good."

"Did you tip the bouncer and wish him a good night."

"Yes."

"You see they let you in because your dad is white. That means you're not a nigger."

Now, I get it! He simply doesn't view me as black. That's how he can degrade blacks to my face. But what about Mum? Why marry an African woman if you look down on the race? It doesn't make sense.

The conversation switched from niggers to the dubious reputation of filthy Arabs who weren't welcome in Blankenberge, or Belgium for that matter. The tense racial discussion lasted till sunrise, ending with the topic of my pathetic, alcoholic slut of a mother, Rudy, and the jealous Jean-Pierre. Of course, we talked about *l'education sexuelle*—again.

Oui, Papa. Oui, Papa. Oui, Papa.

Summer rose and set. Autumn fell. Winter blanketed the town with a British-like grey. A new pessimistic year dawned upon us.

Come February 1982, I had survived my first three-hundred-and-sixty-five days in Belgium. Another reminder that life would not hold me back, regardless of what it threw at me. Meanwhile, a group called The Human League got their first number one hit on the British TV show, *Top of the Pops*. The song was called, "Don't you want me". I related all too well to the title.

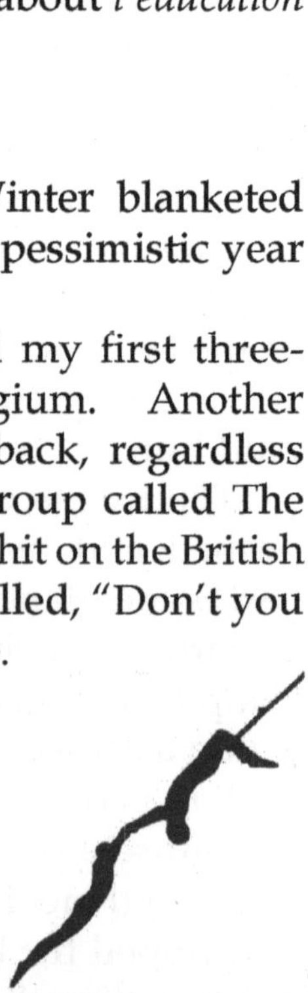

CHAPTER 38

Dad's isolation tactics mellowed. Marcella's visits to my room were few and far between. Mireille and I went back and forth as usual. I blended into the dysfunction of the Jacob family way of living, as one of them, and adapted to Belgian life. I made a few friends, whom I kept at a safe distance fearing they'd see right through me and my dark, dirty secrets of shame and regret.

If only I could escape back to England.

Where would I go? The home? JP? Bollocks I'm trapped.

Either way, I hoped to visit soon, someway, somehow, if only to pick up my record player, vinyl collection and subbuteo game. Long live music and soccer – my saviors.

My French became fluent, my Dutch reasonable. The Under Seventeen soccer team moved me up to the reserves and occasional first team spot. Dad policed my training much to my dislike. He forced me to lift weights in the privacy of our home, which was a good thing, because I was so skinny and weak. A little more meat on my frame would add to my game.

He reveled in my hard earned soccer success and turned it into his vicarious triumph. I no longer played for me, but for him. I despised him for that.

He embarrassed me at matches with his zealous support, referee insulting, and hand-holding with Mireille. People commented beneath their breath about their "unique" relationship.

Posters of Michael Jackson and Manchester United covered the walls of my attic bunker. I asked regularly for permission to visit England. The answer remained no, followed by a lengthy disclaimer as to why there was no need.

"I know, *Papa*. You're right, but it would be nice to pick up my belongings, especially my records and record player. You know how much I love music."

"For how long?"

That answer took me by surprise.

Was he serious?

"Eh, three to five days, or so. I can't imagine needing to stay longer. Oh, you and Mireille are gonna' love my record collection."

"Perhaps," he replied, uninterested.

"Especially Michael Jackson. He's brilliant." I added.

They'd never heard of him.

"What about Jean-Pierre, son?"

"I'm gonna tell him I never want to talk to him again. He's not my brother. He betrayed me."

"Yes, he did. I'm glad you see that now."

He agreed to let me visit. My chance to escape.

CHAPTER 39

I stayed with JP and his wife, Janice, for a short week during the Easter holidays, feeling hypocritical. I both loved and hated my brother and had lied to Dad.

"You've filled out some, and grown a little bit, too, V. Must be all those waffles," JP said. "So, you're all of four foot two now."

"Shut up, John. I'll be taller than you in a couple more years and a few more waffles."

His wife welcomed me with open arms and lovely dishes from her native country, Singapore.

"This is lovely, Janice," I said.

"Plenty more where that came from."

I remained polite, never taking seconds unless asked, which she always did, placing an extra serving on my plate before she even finished her customary sentence. "Best to eat it and not let it go to waste. It'll be an insult if you don't eat my food."

No matter how much I ate, the fridge always seemed full of delicious curried nosh with other irresistible Far East spices.

JP and I talked plenty about Dad. Sometimes, all day and all night till the following morning. Janice was very understanding, allowing us plenty of private time to catch up.

The conversations fueled my doubts, provoked my

suspicions, and aggravated my hate of my father. JP referred to Dad as Jackie, a nickname Mum had given him, for unknown reasons to us. In my mind, he was no longer my dad but a lying, manipulative bastard I wanted to punch in the gob. I, too, would address him as Jackie when I got home.

"So, why go back if it's that bad?" JP asked.

"Don't know. Maybe to honor Mum's dying wish and take care of my little sister, Mireille."

Mum's dying wish was the most important responsibility I carried, and I would die before failing to honor it.

"You know he's lying. She's not Mum's daughter! Mum was never pregnant after you."

She had to have been. It's too big of a lie.

"JP, Mireille even has the same identical handwriting as Mum."

"So bloody what?"

What to believe. Was JP jealous, as Dad had suggested, or was Dad the liar my instinct and brother told me he was?

"Has he ever tried anything, V?"

"Like what."

"You know why he went to jail. Don't play stupid."

"No. No, of course not." If only JP knew how desperate I was to vent all that had happened to relieve my own guilt. "He doesn't treat Marcella and Grandma very well. That's about it, really."

He nodded, inviting me to talk more. I did.

"They're like his servants with no right to speak unless asked to confirm his stories."

"Exactly how I remember him. He got spoiled in Zaire with all Mum's servants. They hated him cause he abused them. I don't think you should go back."

"Why would I want to go back to Zaire?" I said with a cheeky grin.

"Very funny, V, you little bugger. Back to Belgium."

I had learned to use humor as a tool to diffuse tough or sad situations. It worked perfectly in this instance, giving me a light-hearted breather and a cue to change the subject before I opened up and revealed my darkest shame.

Janice interrupted us. "You guys hungry?"

I couldn't insult her cooking, let alone resist. After a quick feast, the conversation resumed in private.

"What happened to your school friend, Okee, or something?" JP asked.

"You mean, Oku? Don't know. Never spoke to him again after leaving. Pretty sad, in it?"

"Do you know where he lives?"

"Don't have his address or number. I'm gonna go to Howard's Lane tomorrow to pick up my stuff and say hi to whoever still lives there. If Ricky Dees is still there, he might have heard from Oku."

"I'll give you a lift. Call me when you need me to come pick you up."

Ricky and I had lived in the home together for a good six years. We had enjoyed a great sporting rivalry and a brother-like bond. He was a couple of years younger than me and also a half-caste. I saved his life once when a group of kids and a staff member went skating on a frozen pond. The polar evening stroll there had our toes and fingers numb.

Ricky fell into a hole, glacial water up to his neck, and a deathly panic in his eyes. I hurried to him without thinking the ice might crack and take me down, too. I pulled him out. By the time we got home, after a long walk and a bus ride in the subzero temperatures, he had literally turned purple and blue, but remained alive.

Luckily, he was still at the home when I got there to pick up the remainder of my belongings. The sneaky sod had even claimed my clothes, and my old attic room was now his. It reinforced how forgettable we all were. NEXT!

My record player sat atop a table in the corner of his room. I let him keep my clothes, even my favorite jacket I'd worn to JP's wedding, but the music had to come back with me to Belgium. I lived through music and felt dead without it.

That night Ricky, other kids from the home, and I walked the streets and hung out with some of my old neighborhood friends. We caught up on the good old times and talked about what we all wanted to become.

"I'm gonna come back and play for Man United, get married, and have a family," I said.

Another kid from the home told us he would never have kids. "The world's too cruel to kids, you know what I mean?" Everybody acknowledged his statement. "Look at us lot. Bloody Rejects United, that's what we are. We're all we av." He wished me luck, nonetheless, and reminded me to enjoy the chocolate.

"Cheers, mate. Oy, Ricky, do you remember my friend Oku, from Salesian's? Tall, half-caste guy with a short Afro."

"Yeah, yeah. I see him every now and again in Clapham. He always asks about ya'."

I jotted my address into his diary.

"Give it to Oku next time you see 'm. Cheers, mate."

With my record player and vinyls parceled, JP came and picked me up. It was a long drive to and from his house on Streatham Hill in Lambeth. Like a good Catholic boy, I felt guilty that he had gone out of his way for me.

The next night would be my last in England. JP and I went out and played snooker for several hours. He smoked and drank beer in the dimly lit room as we talked and talked.

"Why do you smoke and drink so much?" I asked.

"Ah, I don't know." He sunk a red ball, followed by the blue, continuing his answer as he walked around the table with his cigarette between his lips. "Why do you care, anyway? They're my lungs."

"Don't you know that's what killed Mum? It doesn't make you look cool, if that's what you think."

"I don't need to try and look cool, V, I am. Besides, I can give it up tomorrow if I want."

"Get lost you can." He sunk another red, and sipped on his pint. "Then, why don't ya?"

He missed the black, leaving the white ball too far for me to reach.

"You smoke at least twenty a day," I said.

"I only smoke when I go out. A couple of fags here and there."

"A couple? Bollocks. You're addicted, just like Mum." I walked to the white ball, evaluating my shot. Options weren't good. I placed one leg up onto the table, stretching across a few balls unable to reach the white one.

"Can you hand me the extension, mate?"

JP laughed at how the stick was bigger than me, and the table way above my waist. I hated being so short. I missed the shot, eventually losing the game, which only added to my growing frustration with JP.

We stepped outside into the stony winter air and walked toward his car.

"Your old banger better start." It didn't—typical. "When are you gonna' buy a bleedin' car that actually works, John?"

"No big deal; I can fix it."

He always said that, but none of his cars ever worked regularly in all the years I'd known him to drive. It pissed his wife off, too. I waited inside the arctic vehicle while he tinkered under the bonnet. We drove home an hour later.

"This thing better start tomorrow, John, so I can get to the station on time."

"No problem, V; I fixed it, didn't I?"

With sadness in my heart, I packed into the wee hours, dreading the return to Belgium. Of course, the car didn't start straight away the next morning.

"Bloody ell, I thought you said you fixed it."

"It's running now, in it?"

We gabbed more during the drive through South London, across Vauxhall Bridge to Victoria Station, which stood around the corner from Buckingham Palace.

"I don't wanna to go back."

"Then don't."

"And then what? I can't go back to the home. Besides, what if Mireille *is* my sister."

"She's not, for Pete's sake."

"Shut up, John. What if there's a one percent chance? And what if it's true that Mum's dying wish was for me to be reunited? Oh, I bloody forgot, you don't give a shit about Mum! Never did, did ya? Or are you jealous I've actually got a dad?"

The discussion escalated and fizzled, resolving nothing. As always, my big brother showed no emotion. Nonetheless, I regretted my comment, knowing it must have hurt.

We sat in silence for the remaining miles. He smoked. I stared out the window. We barely made it in time for me to catch the boat-train to Dover, leaving no chance for an emotional good-bye. He slipped me a few quid hidden in his handshake before I legged it to buy my ticket.

The ferry across the Channel to Ostend was lonely and empty. I wanted to swim back to England, but I needed answers and understanding so remained seated, fighting the roll of the sea.

Would they hold me back again at Belgian customs for being black? Yes, they did. Would this racism ever end?

My dad's white, for Pete's sake. Don't you know what that means?

CHAPTER 40

Dad, Mireille, and Marcella picked me up in Ostend late afternoon. It seemed so long since my initial arrival at this same port one cold, dark, winter morning a year ago.

"Hello, son."

"*Bonjour, —*" I replied, as if trapped in a frozen pond unable to utter the name, Jackie.

Not much was said during the thirty-minute drive home. My answers to his questions were short, avoiding any form of self-incrimination. "Yes. No. Not really." What I really wanted to say was, "Jackie, you lying prick, I know the truth!"

All the kids were happy to see me. "*Allez, Tonton, allez, Tonton!*"

We convened in the living room. Mireille sat on her dad's lap with her head resting on his shoulders and neck. Grandma sat quietly in the other armchair. I sat in the middle of the sofa surrounded by my younger siblings. As long as they were not in bed, I wouldn't experience the anticipated Gestapo interrogation. I should have paid attention to the cliché, always expect the unexpected.

Jackie told Mireille to get up from his lap. "Quiet children," he blubbered, before standing in the middle of the living room. He rubbed his beard and aligned his spectacles.

"So, *Tonton,* why don't you tell us all about the *lies* your jealous brother said about me, and don't *lie!*"

I *lied* like I'd never done before and talked about everything else other than what he fished for, including how I wanted to call him Jackie and not Dad.

"Did you know that your brother was a breach birth, *Tonton?* He came out feet first almost ripping out your precious mother's insides."

I nodded, remaining quiet.

"Do you know what they say in Africa about children born feet first?"

I shrugged my shoulders.

"They are cursed and evil. Ask anybody." He peered at Marcella. "Do I speak the truth?"

"*Oui,*" she said.

"Mireille, am I lying?"

"Of course not, *Papa*. That's the truth."

What did my sister know? What did Marcella know about African culture? What did I know?

He went on. "I'm aware that Jean-Pierre corrupted you with lies. He's evil and envious of you. Your mum was afraid of him. Ask Grandma, she knows." He pleaded to her with a soft voice. "*Bobonne,* do you remember what Regine always said about Jean-Pierre, how he was a cursed child?"

"It's been too long for me to remember. I'm too old now. So sorry. How is Regine?"

"Are you mocking me? She's dead!"

"Oh, that's right, what a shame. Sweet lady." She pointed to the grandfather clock. "I think it's my bedtime."

"Yes, it's everybody's," he announced. "Children! Marcella, take them up. And some decaf would be nice."

He helped Grandma up to her feet and kissed her gently on the cheek. "I love you, *Maman.*"

When she kissed me, her frail hand squeezed mine as if to say, be strong. I knew she was on my side.

"Tea, *Tonton?*" Marcella asked on her way out.

"*Oui. Merci.*"

Dad told Marcella to hurry and not fuss. "Poor *Bobonne*. She's getting old you know. Such a brave woman."

She must have been to raise you!

"She forgets. But she knew all too well about Jean-Pierre."

Marcella came back and served the hot beverages, spilling some onto the white lace atop the coffee table.

"You stupid, clumsy imbecile!" Dad yelled. "Can't you do anything right?"

She said nothing other than emit a sigh and cleaned up. He lectured on. I struggled to keep my eyes open from tiredness, let alone my ears from disinterest.

"Your mum feared Jean-Pierre would harm her one day. Ask Rudy if you don't believe me." How convenient for Jackie that Rudy lived somewhere in America and I had lost contact. The conversation went on and on.

"He needs sleep," Marcella said.

"What do you know, woman? And why are you always protecting him?"

"I'm not!"

"Don't you dare raise your voice!"

It was unlike Marcella to offer any resistance. I could sense she'd had enough of his suppression and manipulation, too. She softened her tone.

"Look, Mireille is falling asleep, too. It's almost one in the morning and *Tonton* has soccer tomorrow."

Marcella had saved me.

The next few days were strangely peaceful. No interrogation, no isolation—no drama! Then came Wednesday, the habitual half day at school, without soccer practice as an evening escape.

"I spoke with Jean-Pierre on the phone this morning," Dad announced during lunch. "I am ashamed of you, son."

"Why? I didn't do anything."

"If your mother hadn't been too busy drinking and sleeping around with police commissioners, she might have paid more attention to your upbringing."

"What did I do?"

Dad mumbled with a mouthful of soggy ham and cheese sandwich he had dipped into his coffee—a habit I hated.

"He said that you kept raiding the fridge without offering to pay toward groceries."

I couldn't believe my ears. Why had my brother betrayed me like that? A combination of anger, emptiness, and defeat danced within me, as if my soul had been sent to hell and condemned to eternal aloneness and rejection. Jean-Pierre was my final pillar of strength and hope, no more. Me against life and the world.

Janice insisted I eat, saying it would be an insult not to. What a load of bollocks.

"I wasn't there, *Tonton*. You tell me. Did you go in the fridge and eat all their food?"

"No. Well, yes, kind of, but—"

"Well, there you go. I can't be making it up if I wasn't there. It's your brother's story, not mine."

You lying bastard, John.

"And what's this about making your brother drive you around London late at night like a chauffeur?" He dipped his sandwich again. Small chunks of lost bread floated in his cup. "You didn't even propose to pay for gas."

You backstabbing git. Why, John? I hate you!

Dad was right. Breach birth children are truly cursed and evil. Even Rudy had argued that fact, too. I half remembered Mum doing Voodoo rituals with us when younger. She slit the throats of pigeons, draining their thick, crimson blood into a bowl while chanting. We sipped the warm viscose fluid and ate strange rocky substances, reciting words in Swahili. She said it was to protect us. It now made sense—protect us from the curse that was my evil, breach-birth brother. My father wasn't a liar, after all. JP was. *Sorry, Jackie. I mean, Dad.*

You'll never betray me again, John. Nobody will. I'll never talk to you for as long as I live.

CHAPTER 41

With Jean-Pierre out of the picture, my father had me cornered, tamed, and at his mercy. A different reality emerged. What once appeared to be a loving couple proved to be very much otherwise. Marcella and Dad hated each other. I felt guilty to have caused the riff until Marcella confessed that they already hated each other before my arrival.

"We pretended, so we could give you the image of a loving home," she said. "There is no healthy love in this place. Everything is broken. You brought hope, *Tonton.*"

Dad no longer hid behind pretense. "What was I thinking when I made you the stupid mother of my children?" he'd often say.

She shrugged it off as if immune, or through lack of self-dignity and ability to stand up for herself. I looked down on her for that, even though I suffered from the same ailment.

I learned to get along with my father by saying yes. Spending all my time in my room listening to music facilitated the feigned relationship. I practiced Michael Jackson moves hours on end. I'd be on stage like him one day, reveling in love, applause, and admiration.

Another year passed with many new discoveries and realizations. We were poor. Dad rarely worked, bringing in a meager unemployment check. Marcella only worked during the seasonal months as a waitress at a holiday resort, pulling unemployment for the remainder of the year. I worked another summer washing dishes, giving my skimpy earnings to my father. Nightclubs still turned me away.

I met my first girlfriend that year at school and lost my virginity at the age of eighteen—late compared to all my friends. Despite years of *l'education sexuelle*, I'd never had intercourse before. This fact does not lighten the burden of my inner disgust and guilt of my sexual experiences.

Her name was Maureen, a very crude, sexually experienced girl from a neighboring village called *Uitkerke*.

"Go and buy condoms and come by the house tonight at eight," she ordered me.

The anticipation and pressure was unbearable. I humiliated myself and performed poorly that night due to a mental block. Sexuality felt dirty. Nonetheless, I experienced the inside of a woman for the first time.

In due time, the mental block and disgust of intimacy passed. A sense of liberation and cleansing came with the relationship.

We dated for about eight months. She spoke neither English nor French, which helped improve my Dutch. School grades improved drastically. Maybe I could overcome this language barrier and actually graduate one day, albeit a minimum of four years later than normal.

Just three more to go.

I maintained a solitary life at home and in public, keeping friends at a safe distance, and didn't miss England as much. The pain of Mum's death had faded. As for Jean-Pierre and Rudy, they were a forgotten part of my life that belonged to yesterday. I needed to overcome today and tomorrow, which I was determined to do.

Every now and again, I'd spend an evening with the family and watch a film or something to appease Dad's consistent requests for my company. Tonight was such a night, an unforgettable one.

The family gathered in the living room when my

youngest sister snitched and announced that our brother, Christophe, was in pain.

"His willie hurts," she said.

"What's the matter, Christophe?" Dad asked.

A very embarrassed brother eventually admitted that his penis was swollen.

"Let me see," said Dad. Christophe tried to avoid revealing himself. "Pull your pants down and show me what's wrong. There's no shame in this house."

From my chair, I could see that the head of his penis sat wedged within his foreskin.

"We have to release it," Dad said. "Mireille, get me some Vaseline and cotton swabs."

After several attempts to lubricate, Dad concluded that the only solution was to induce an erection. He told Mireille to arouse her younger brother using the Vaseline and her hands.

This is not happening. Please, God.

Mireille seemed astonished, but giggled and played along.

Marcella questioned Jackie. "Are you serious?"

"Do you have any other solutions?" he barked. "I'm trying to help my son, that I love, so stay out of this. Maybe you don't love our children, but I do."

I headed toward the door. Dad ordered me back. "You need to stay and watch this! It might happen to your children one day. In fact, everybody needs to look and learn."

Mireille applied the Vaseline. Christophe sat in the chair embarrassed and in pain. He did not react to the stimulation.

"Well, well, well, Mireille. Don't you know how to arouse a man? How on earth will you take care of your future husband?" Dad asked and laughed. The children tittered along. "You'll have to use your mouth. Maybe you'll be better at that," he joked further.

I had reluctantly accepted that all families probably participated in *l'education sexuelle,* but this was surely beyond any form of education. I observed Marcella, who had accepted the funny of the whole scene. Grandma stared straight ahead as if denying her own presence. Disgust and indignation ran through my veins.

I have to get away. Run!

"Well, Mireille, you're a real zero," commented one of the siblings, evoking mass hysteria.

"Shut up; I bet you can't do any better," said Mireille.

Dad invited the others to do just that. Excitement bounced off the walls. Vomit formed in my throat.

Our Father, Who art in heaven….

Run! Leave!

I had no money and nowhere to go!

Doesn't matter. Just run! Why didn't you jump off that ferry and swim back to England when you had the chance?

God, please turn back the clock! Mum, give me the power of your Voodoo. Is anybody bloody listening? God? I hate You. Take my life already.

A few days later, Christophe, at the young age of nine, was partially circumcised and scarred for life. We all were.

CHAPTER 42

Report him!

Who do I tell? They won't believe me!

What will happen to my siblings? They'll be sent to homes like I was – ridiculed. They don't deserve that. Worse still, they don't deserve this!

Report him!

But nobody will have the courage to testify against him. It will be my word against his. He'll walk free. I lose. We all lose.

Still, I must report him! I can't.

All I can do is bear the burden of this cross for the rest of my life, in silence.

Where are you, God? There is no God, no justice, only hell!

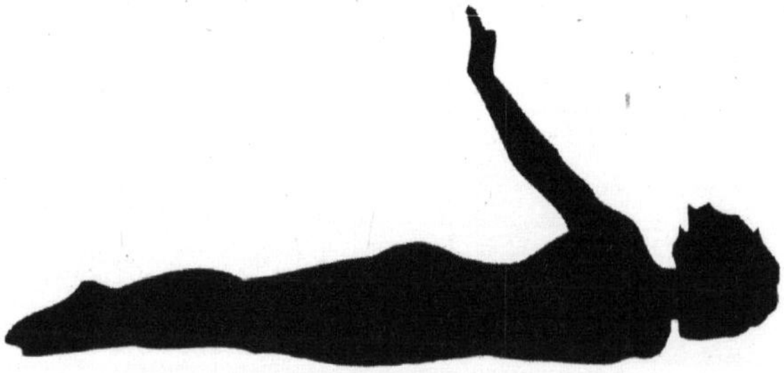

CHAPTER 43

The sight and sound of my father made me itch, as if rampant ants danced all over my skin. The smell of his breath when he kissed me on the cheek made me want to rinse my face with Dettol. The never disappearing visual of my sister's head between my nine-year-old brother's naked legs haunted me.

I hated Dad for his perversions. I hated Belgium for its racism, Marcella for her weakness, and life for being so cruel.

My profound disgust turned each conversation with my father into an argument. My hairs stood on end like that of a pissed-off cat, claws on red alert at each word, all of which I challenged.

Marcella gained strength through my resistance. The fear he had instilled in me lingered, however. I remained bunkered in my attic.

A day or two later, on another freezing winter evening, he surprised me and knocked at my door.

"Are you avoiding me, son?" Keeping my attention on the TV, I raised my eyebrows and shrugged my shoulders. "Very well, then." He calmly walked across the room to the TV and turned it off.

I sprang from the sleeper-couch, switched on the stereo and blasted a Michael Jackson record, humming along in defiance.

"Don't make me confiscate your music."

"You can't touch my records. I brought those from

England. Paid for with my money, not yours."

"I own everything here."

He unplugged the record player and walked out of the room with it. Five minutes later he barged back in. "Who's stubborn now?"

"You call that stubborn? I call that immature."

My disrespectful comment pushed his explode button.

"Who the fuck do you think you are, you little piece of British phlegmatic shit."

He stepped to the wall and ripped down the Manchester United poster.

"I AM THE MASTER OF THIS HOUSE!" Spittle flew from his mouth. His eyes bulged from the pressure.

He reminded me of Hitler during a zealous speech.

"I want all this African crap on your walls gone! And all those, too," he said, pointing to the pictures of Mum, Jean-Pierre, and Rudy on my nightstand. "You'll be gone, too, if you don't obey."

He shut off the gas heater and slammed the door behind him.

I sat in cold silence for the remainder of the night, thinking. By morning, everything that reminded me of who I *was,* and my heritage, came down. Only an isolated picture of Mum remained.

Breakfast was quiet and awkward. My father always slept in, so I didn't have to deal with him until lunch, which arrived all too quickly.

He didn't hesitate and fired away at the dining table.

"Did you take down what I asked?"

I nodded.

"What about your precious mother's picture?"

Everybody held their breath in anticipation.

"Answer me!"

I would not give him the pleasure, thinking, *Up yours* 'Dad.'

"So, you didn't. What's wrong with you? Your mother was a fucking alcoholic whore incapable of raising children."

He took a sharp swig of coffee, wiped his mouth with his hand, and signaled to Marcella for a refill.

"How can you love and protect your mother so much? She was weak and selfish, a failure, a fucking whore. Do you hear me, Vital Jacob? A whore. How can you love her?"

He paused as if truly expecting an answer. I held my silence.

"How can you love a woman that made you sleep in the hallway so she could suck another man's dick for money?"

He had never gone this far with his insults. He slammed his hand onto the tabletop shaking everything on it.

"HOW?"

The house trembled. The children, I now begrudged for being an extension of him, shuddered with panic plastered over their blameless faces. Mireille sat expressionless. Grandma sympathetically blinked both eyes at me—her way of giving me strength.

After the echo of his rage faded into the walls, his nostrils enlarged, emitting heavy sighs. He slid his dark black spectacles back up onto the bridge of his nose and looked vacantly into my eyes. Beads of sweat sprouted on his forehead.

He looked over to Marcella for backup. None came. Mireille shrugged her shoulders and frowned. He collected himself and changed his tone to one with charm and tenderness.

"My dear son, the only reason why you suffered as a child was because of your mother. She let you down, I won't. Oh, *mon pauvre fils*, my poor son."

I held on tight to my cloak of civil resistance.

"I love you, *Tonton*, more than you can ever imagine, unconditionally."

His declaration of unconditional love almost made me melt. The nickname, *Tonton*, always evoked feelings of comfort, love, and security, touching my heart at its most vulnerable core, yet, I refused to give in. The desperate raging manipulator reemerged.

"I said, how, Vital Jacob. She was an alcoholic slut. A Ho."

Each verbal blow against Mum smashed into my face like a Mike Tyson punch. My legs wobbled, but I remained upright. The bell rang, but the fight did not end.

Seconds away, round two.

"She abandoned you; I love and spoil you. What did your slut of a mother ever do for you?" He glanced over at Marcella. "Tell me I'm wrong."

"She wasn't a good mother, this is true. *Tonton*, it's all for your own--."

"Enough," he told Marcella. She retreated into her frail broken shell of shame.

Round three.

"Her Guinness was more important than you ever were. Your mother wasn't even capable of breast-feeding you she was so full of junk. She was an alcoholic whore. What was your mother? ANSWER ME!"

After he slandered Mum's name beyond the reputation of *Mary Magdalene*, I answered.

"My mother was an alcoholic whore," I said with a defeated murmur. "A slut." My head sank into my chest.

I sniffled with humiliation. My brother and sisters stared at me, confusion written all over their faces. He had won the fight, the battle and the war. Marcella looked stunned, Grandma shell-shocked. Mireille looked down at the floor. My lungs expanded, drawing in a breath of strength.

You're not my father.

The chocolate milk turned sour and grey, the air poisonous. I lost my appetite.

You're not my father.

A hot flash blanketed my head, followed by a wave of cold dizziness. He wore an expression of inner content hidden behind his beard. It angered me. He stood up and held out his arms. "Son."

Did he expect me to crumble and fall into his open arms begging for his love and forgiveness?

You're not my father. You're not my father. You're not my father.

From behind my wall of grief, a wave of boldness possessed me. I wiped my tears and stood up.

"Okay, Mr. Eugene Jacob, you listen to me."

His face revealed total astonishment.

Fifteenth and final round.

"You're not my father. I am ashamed to be your son."

His arms dropped, as did his jaw.

"I will love my mother forever and will never love you."

I glanced down at my sandwich knife in contemplation of what I could do with it. Instead of stabbing and killing him with it, I headed for the door. As I walked by him, he attempted to hug and console me. I barged my way past his extended arms. Time to go for the knock out punch.

"Go to hell you racist bastard. Black is beautiful and I'm glad Mum left you. I wish you'd succeeded when you slit your wrists. I'm glad you got arrested in England. And by the way, Belgium soccer sucks."

I left the room and slammed the door and paused for a moment, wondering if I should go back and use the sandwich knife anyway, or walk up to my bedroom and lock the door and hide forever.

The first step seemed impossible. The weight of the anger and self-loathing in my heart paralyzed me.

How could you call Mum a whore?

My right foot lifted the concrete block chained to it, up to the second step.

Chère Maman, please forgive me. I didn't mean it. You're not a whore. I would have died for you and switched places. Forgive me. I love you, Mum.

My left foot moved a little less encumbered up the next stair, then the right more easily. At each upward stride, my soul inhaled a small ray of sunlight. I floated up to the attic level on a carpet of optimism and redemption. My bedroom door opened, as if by magic, compelling me to enter a different, bright, and promising dimension, a new chapter.

I placed the *Thriller* LP onto the record player, turned up the volume, and danced, danced, danced.

Just beat it, Dad!

I pirouetted, grabbed my crotch, stood on my toes and moonwalked all night long with joy. I had no idea that one day the dance would propel me to run away with the circus, but not just any circus. Cirque Du Soleil!

With such a strong feeling of victory filling my spirit, I couldn't wait for tomorrow and live up to the name my Mum gave me. I am VITAL. I am full of life. The world became mine to make of it what I chose.

Choice!

The sweet, naïve *Tonton* died that day and became a man, ready to fly and face the perils of adult life, with or without a net. I decided to live life on my terms from here on out and become my own person. I knew it would not be easy, but knew that I could and would, even though still trapped in my father's prison 'til, at least, my twenty-first birthday. Just two-and-a-half years more.

Racism would not hold me back. My past would not hold me back. My father would not hold me back.

Nothing will.

Bring it!

THE END

"By all means, don't say if I can, say I WILL."
Abraham Lincoln

Vital left Europe to pursue his dreams. He performed in Cirque du Soleil's *Mystère* and *Quidam*. He studied literature and fine art at UNLV and the College of Southern Nevada. When he is not writing, choreographing or painting, Vital is a public speaker—a modern-day renaissance man. For more info, log onto *www.VitalGermaine.com.*